DEATH IN PHILADELPHIA

DEATH IN PHILADELPHIA

THE MURDER OF KIMBERLY ERNEST

THOM NICKELS

AMERICA
THROUGH TIME®
ADDING COLOR TO AMERICAN HISTORY

For Detective Tom Augustine and Dorothe Ernest

Fonthill Media Inc.
www.fonthillmedia.com
office@fonthillmedia.com

First published 2023

ISBN 978-1-63499-458-3

Typeset in Mrs Eaves XL Serif Narrow
Printed and bound in England

Do this in remembrance of me: the solution, then, or so such pervasive fantasies suggested, was to partake of the symbolic body and blood of The Jogger, whose idealization was by this point complete, and was rendered, significantly, in details stressing her "difference," or superior class. The Jogger was someone who wore, according to Newsday, "a light gold chain around her slender neck" as well as, according to the News, a "modest" gold ring and "a thin sheen" of lipstick. The Jogger was someone who would not, according to the Post, "even dignify her alleged attackers with a glance." The Jogger was someone who spoke, according to the News, in accents "suited to boardrooms," accents that might therefore seem "foreign to many native New Yorkers." In her first appearance on the witness stand she had been subjected, the Times noted, "to questions that most people do not have to answer publicly during their lifetimes," principally about her use of a diaphragm on the Sunday preceding the attack, and had answered these questions, according to an editorial in the News, with an "indomitable dignity" that had taught the city a lesson "about courage and class."

From *'Sentimental Journeys' (the 1989 Central Park Jogger Case)* by Joan Didion

CONTENTS

INTRODUCTION: A BACKDROP OF MURDERS

"This case is different," said Sgt. Paul Musi, who worked on the case. "For some reason, Philadelphia embraces this girl."

In 1990, I had just moved to a second-story apartment near the corner of 21st and Pine Streets when I opted to take an evening stroll along Market Street, where I was then accosted by a group of four or five youths who stole my (empty) wallet and ripped my jeans so badly I had to cover myself as I scurried home. I had never been mugged by a group of people before, so I was pretty well shaken. Time passed. I got over it.

The number of homicides in Philadelphia in 1990 numbered 500, a statistic often compared to 2021's murder rate (550 and counting). Center City in 1990 was not exactly a hotbed of mass shootings. In fact, on the surface, life there seemed relatively peaceful and calm. Still, 1990 was the year that most city residents became aware of the growing homeless problem in the city. The homeless, who were called "bag people" or panhandlers, generally congregated near 13th and Chestnut Streets, and stories about "bag people" were common in the local press. There was the elderly "Duck Lady," for instance, who would lift her dress and relieve herself in the middle of Chestnut Street. Random shootings—the kind we have become accustomed to today—tended to occur in the neighborhoods. Center City, on the other hand, seemed to be a magnet for other sorts of crimes, like the 1995 murder of Center City jogger Kimberly Ernest (the subject of this book) and the scandal surrounding Eddie Savitz, or "Uncle Ed," in 1992.

I asked former Philadelphia detective Tom Augustine (now deceased), noted for his role in the booking of Richard Wise and Herbert Haak in the Kimberly Ernest case, what he could recall about the city's homicides in 1990. Augustine told me he could not recall much and confirmed my recollection that most of the homicides then occurred in the neighborhoods rather than downtown. The year 1990 would prove to be a gateway because the years preceding it and the years after would put Philadelphia on the map for a number of sensational crimes and news events. In 1985, for instance, there was the MOVE bombing fiasco. One year later, the Gary M. Heidnik murders shocked the city, while another serial killer, Harrison Graham, was charged with killing seven women. In the five years from 1985 to 1990, the Frankford Slasher, who was never caught, also killed seven women.

The two most sensational and tragic murders that attracted international attention were the death by brutal beating of sixteen-year-old Eddie Polec by six teens in Northeast Philadelphia in 1994 and the murder of gay artist Anthony Milano of Levittown in 1987.

Milano, aged twenty-six, was on his way home from a Bible study class when he stopped at the Edgley Inn in Tullytown for a beer and a sandwich. There he met Richard Laird and Frank Chester, who had been at the bar for some time and were very drunk. Sometime after 2 a.m., Laird and Chester forced Milano to drive them home. The three drove for about an hour to a rural area, where Milano was ordered out of the car, beaten, and his throat slit multiple times with a box cutter.

I covered the Milano trial in Doylestown and sat close to the killers in the press section. Throughout the trial, I made it a point to study the expressions on the two men's faces. The look on Frank Chester's face suggested some remorse, while Richard Laird maintained a look of arrogance, as if he would gladly kill Milano again if given the chance. I also had the opportunity to speak to Milano's parents, Vito and Rose (now deceased), who sat together looking thoroughly broken-hearted during a court recess in an obscure section of the courthouse. Both Laird and Chester were found guilty of first-degree murder and sentenced to death, although, over the years, the men have argued their case before a number of judges and have had the verdict reversed on technicalities. Both were retried. Laird is still sentenced to death, while Chester was sentenced to life in prison with no chance of parole.

Three years later, 1990 saw the first arrest of "Uncle Ed," or "Fast Eddie," who would make international headlines two years later when his Wanamaker House apartment was raided by police. Eddie Savitz was a 1963 University of Penn graduate and an actuary in his family's firm and was by all accounts a well-liked and talented gentleman despite a suicidal penchant for teenage and underage boys, especially from Roman Catholic and Bishop Neumann high schools. After his initial arrest in 1990 (and eventual not-guilty charge) for purchasing men's soiled underwear, the high volume of teenage boy traffic in and out of his Center City apartment caused Alan Domb, then president of the homeowners association there, to alert police. With the help of neighbors, police wiretapped and installed a hidden video camera inside Savitz's apartment, where they observed the goings-on for six months.

I happened to be walking along Walnut Street when police raided Savitz's apartment, so I joined the crowd of curious pedestrians who watched as innumerable police vans and media trucks pulled up in front of the building. At the time, I assumed there had been a murder inside the building and was surprised when I learned that the bust had to do with sex with underage boys, strange scatological fetishes, and an AIDS scare that added fuel to the raging paranoia about AIDS that was sweeping the city.

Police wiretaps revealed that "Uncle Ed" received 2,925 calls from teenage boys between December 6 and March 6, 1992. News reports at the time revealed that "Uncle Ed" did not have sex with all the boys he saw; he employed some to do household chores. For many boys, visiting "Uncle Ed" was a rite of passage. Many of the boys' fathers had also visited "Uncle Ed" as teens when they needed spare cash.

What largely propelled "Uncle Ed's" arrest was the AIDS crisis, which in 1990 still inspired a lot of fear. Although Savitz would in fact die of AIDS-related complications, ironically not one of the thousands of his contacts did. Misconceptions about how AIDS was transmitted were very common then. Medical literature blithely stated that "sex between men" was a risk factor (as well as sharing needles in the case of addicts) without the mention of any specificity at all. But as Philadelphia playwright Samuel R. Delany noted in his book *Solids and Surds*: "Thus, sexual acts from French kissing to fellatio do not transmit the virus, with or without ejaculation. Tales that include 'sex' must be told with a specificity at such a level, or, by definition, they are encouraging the ignorance that spreads AIDS."

The Savitz case had a profound effect on the fear of AIDS and on "AIDS carriers" (homosexuals) in the city. After Savitz's arrest, I had many experiences of being called an "AIDS carrier" as I walked with my partner along Walnut or Chestnut Street. DA Lynne Abraham was criticized at the time for tapping into this fear. AIDS panic was so bad in Philadelphia, it caused the *New York Times* to report:

Not since 1985, when a police confrontation with the armed cult Move left 61 houses in flames and killed 11 people, has Philadelphia been so shaken. More than a thousand people have called the District Attorney's office and AIDS counselors about the Savitz case to report their own and other people's contacts with Mr. Savitz. There have been scattered threats of violence against homosexuals and organizations that assist people with AIDS, and these organizations have sharply criticized the authorities' handling of the situation, saying they had exaggerated the threat of infection from contact with Mr. Savitz.

In the late 1970s, while working on a feature on male hustlers in Suburban Station for Philadelphia's *The Distant Drummer*, I spotted Eddie Savitz on a number of occasions—a tall man in thick black, horn-rimmed glasses in a long overcoat and in what looked to be a bad hairpiece—standing in the back of the station near the men's room, watching and waiting.

It was also during 1990 that Frank Rizzo ran for mayor as a Republican against Democratic Party nominee Ed Rendell. Rizzo at that time had a radio show on WCAU (AM), where he came down hard on the outgoing Wilson Goode administration. I was able to obtain an interview with Rizzo at the station despite the fact that I had vilified him for years in *The Philadelphia Gay News*, the *South Street Star*, and the *Welcomat*. I was quite nervous meeting him, but he thoroughly disarmed me with his charm. He spent a lot of time talking about a police officer friend of his in the hospital with AIDS. Once again, AIDS and the fear of AIDS seemed to dominate the conversation.

GARY HEIDNIK

It has been decades since serial killer Gary Michael Heidnik was wheeled into the lethal injection room at the State Correctional Institution at Rockview in Centre County, Pennsylvania.

Heidnik, the last person to be put to death by Pennsylvania, was executed on a gurney with a sheet covering most of his body. His last day included a meeting with one of his three children, Maxine Davidson White, a chat with a spiritual advisor, and a final meal of black coffee and two slices of cheese pizza.

The convicted rapist and killer of two women had no final words. Observers noted how after the lethal injection his face turned bright red then went ashen. When his death was announced at 10:29 p.m., a woman in the galley shouted, "Thank you, Jesus!" Among the ten or so witnesses in the room, applause broke out.

Post execution, Heidnik's remains were cremated, although after his death his legacy lived on in the world of crime novels (what is sometimes termed "tragedy porn"), documentary films, podcasts, and as inspiration for the character of Buffalo Bill in the film *The Silence of the Lambs.*

The scene of Heidnik's grisly crimes was his home at 3520 N. Marshall Street in North Philadelphia.

From November 1986 to March 1987, Heidnik kidnapped six women—Josefina Rivera, Sandra Lindsay, Lisa Thomas, Deborah Dudley, Jacqueline Askins, and Agnes Adams—chaining them to pipes in the basement of his house where he deprived them of food and water while beating and raping them daily. Two of the women died in captivity. Sandra Lindsay died after hanging by her wrist from a ceiling beam for almost a week; Deborah Dudley died when Heidnik filled a pit in the basement with water and then forced Josefina Rivera to apply a live electrical wire to the chain shackled to Dudley's body.

Heidnik's fantasy was the creation of a "birthing harem," but to do that he had to have as many children as possible with the women in his basement. Defense Attorney Chuck Peruto, who represented Heidnik in the late 1980s, told 6 ABC in 2019 that Heidnik "wanted to have a perfect race of children from these women."

Heidnik's victims were mostly mentally challenged African American women he met while trolling for prostitutes near Front and Girard (where he met Rivera).

Rivera, Heidnik's first and most "famous" victim, met Heidnik on November 25, 1986. Rivera, who lived at 6th and Girard, says she got "sidetracked" in life when she gave in to a severe weed and cocaine addiction. For Rivera, sex work was an easy way to make extra money.

"I was always on Front Street," she said in one interview. "It was the day before Thanksgiving. It was raining out, cold, there was no traffic, and as I was making my way to Front Street, Gary pulled up in his Cadillac." Rivera, who said that she never went to a client's home, made an exception in the case of Heidnik. "The word 'nut' is not stamped on anybody's head," she said.

After having sex with Heidnik, Rivera says he came up behind her and started to choke her. He put a handcuff on her wrist and put her into a hole in his basement.

Heidnik then put Sandra Lindsay into the hole. "For the first month me and Sandra stayed in there by ourselves," Rivera said. "He would bring us hot chocolate in the morning for breakfast and at night he would bring down maybe two or three hot dogs. He wanted to have a farm and he wanted to have women on the farm. He wanted to have all these kids."

As other women were forced into the basement, Rivera reported that Heidnik developed a system of rules. "When you got a punishment you got bread and water. He would take away all your privileges."

Before the nightmare was over, Heidnik would cook the flesh of one of his victims and mix it with dog food, then feed it to the captives. Rivera eventually worked with Heidnik in what she says was an act of desperation to save the kidnapped women.

What makes a serial killer? That question has haunted experts for years, but the answers are as varied as the style and idiosyncrasies of serial killers themselves.

"Some of the most notorious serial killers of our time have something in common beside their thirst for blood," *Real Crime* reported in 2017. "They were all adopted. David Berkowitz (a.k.a. Son of Sam), Ted Bundy, Aileen Wuornos, Joel Rifkin and the Boston Strangler are just a handful of the prominent serial murderers who also happen to be adoptees."

In 2014, *Scientific American* asked, "Do serial killers have an extra chromosome?" "While there is no such thing as a 'killer gene,'" the article stated, "research is revealing genetic tendencies towards violent behaviour." There are some who believe that serial killers experienced childhood trauma or early separation from their mothers, and as a result of that they learn how to suppress empathy.

Other serial killers have come to be associated with the occult. The Son of Sam wrote letters decorated with satanic symbols. The Zodiac Killer dressed up in ritual garb and made use of the Gnostic cross. Ted Bundy drained blood from his victims and had an interest in Satanism. Jeffrey Dahmer's dream was to build an occult altar; he was also obsessed with the movie *Exorcist III*. Much of Charles Manson's philosophy came from the Church of the Process, an offshoot of Scientology, and the writings of Aleister Crowley. An interest in the occult and Satanism is a prominent feature in the lives of many serial killers.

That does not seem to be the case with Gary Heidnik, at least at first glance.

Born on November 22, 1943 in a suburb of Cleveland, Heidnik's parents divorced in 1946. He was raised by his mother before being handed over to his father, who was then living with his new wife. Life with his father was anything but pleasant. Plagued by chronic bedwetting, young Gary was humiliated as a child when he was made to hang out his urine-stained sheets from his bedroom window. His father also beat him on a regular basis.

Early signs of psychological dysfunction became apparent when the young Heidnik never made eye contact with his fellow students at school. He also had an oddly shaped head, the result of a severe fall from a tree at age six, although the head injury did not seem to affect his near-genius IQ of 148. A good student, he was enrolled in a military academy at fourteen but dropped out at age seventeen to enlist in the U.S. Army. His stay in the army lasted thirteen months, during which he got his GED and became a medic before his transfer to West Germany.

In 1962, he began to experience headaches—quite possibly a delayed reaction from the fall from the tree—blurred vision, nausea, and dizziness. He was prescribed Trifluoperazine and diagnosed with schizoid personality disorder. An honorable discharge from the military followed.

Heidnik then became an LPN, worked at a Department of Veterans Affairs hospital in Coatesville, Pennsylvania (where he was fired for rude behavior to patients). He moved to Philadelphia where he took courses at the University of Pennsylvania. At the time, he attempted suicide multiple times and was committed to psychiatric hospitals.

In October 1971, Heidnik incorporated a church: the United Church of the Ministers of God. He appointed himself as bishop. This inverted misuse of Christianity was perhaps Heidnik's entrée into occult practices—but his real interest was financial. By 1986 his church was wealthy and thriving, with Heidnik conducting Bible services in his house while the chained women were in his basement. Ordinarily Heidnik drowned out the screams of the kidnapped women by playing loud rock music. Perhaps he used gospel music on Sunday to camouflage the women's screams.

Charles F. Gallagher, deputy district attorney, homicide, worked in the DA's office in 1976. Gallagher wrote an extensive court summary on Heidnik's sanity to counter the serial killer's claim of insanity after his arrest in March 1987.

The court document profiles a highly competent manipulator who has always known how to work the system to his advantage. The court summary, in fact, classifies Heidnik as "intelligent, clean, competent and humorous."

The summary details Heidnik's confession to Rivera that if he were ever to get caught, that he "was going to go into the court and act crazy by saluting the judge because somewhere in the law it states that if you act crazy for a certain amount of years, that eventually your case gets thrown out."

Gallagher mentions the photographs of Heidnik taken immediately after his arrest in March 1987.

"There in that first photo after his arrest you can look into his eyes and see the evil," Gallagher said. In other pictures, Heidnik is unkempt with long hair and a beard, looking, as Gallagher says, "Like Rasputin."

"When he was in court everyday he was completely unkempt in that he let his hair and his beard grow wild," Gallagher recalls. "He saluted the judge often. When he filed the insanity defense they also had to file any reports that they got from his psychiatric specialist. Under the law we [the prosecution] had the right to have our own psychiatric expert interview him."

The prosecution's expert, Dr. Robert Sadoff, accompanied Heidnik to the old holding cell room in City Hall after Heidnik's arrest for first-degree murder. Heidnik, who was held without bail, refused to answer any of Dr. Sadoff's questions. At the trial, Gallagher said that a psychologist from the state prison system testified that it was clear that Heidnik was faking an inability to speak.

Heidnik's "other" arrest in 1978 is worth noting.

After his arrest in June of that year by Detective Patrick Devlin, PPD, for rape (changed later to a misdemeanor in 1979), Heidnik was sent to Graterford to serve two and one-half to five years. On his first day at the prison, he claimed to have attempted suicide by swallowing a light bulb. The ruse worked. Heidnik's "insane act" enabled him to be transferred to Graterford's hospital, a much less arduous sentence than the actual prison itself. Psychiatrists there labeled him "mute and catatonic."

"He was brilliant in the fact that he was able to manipulate all of these systems over the years," Gallagher stated. "When he impregnated his mail order bride from the Philippines, Betsy Disto in 1985 [Heidnik met Disto through a matrimonial service in 1983 and they wrote letters until their meeting and marriage in 1985], he kept bringing these women into the house and having sex with them when she was there with the baby."

Disto walked out on Heidnik but refused to testify against him. She did file for child support, though. "When Heidnik had the women in the basement he was in court fighting the fact that he wasn't paying Disto what the court ordered him to pay her for support," Gallagher said.

Heidnik managed to have three children with three different women whom he never enslaved in his basement: Gary Heidnik, Jr., Jesse John Disto, and Maxine Davidson White.

Gallagher says that after Heidnik made himself a bishop he would hunt for parishioners at the McDonald's at 40th and Walnut Streets. Many of the people he met there were from the nearby Elwyn Institute, a school for the mentally challenged. Heidnik would get the people he met to go to services at his home where they would read the Bible, after which he would have sex with the women.

Heidnik's manipulation of the system included persuading the VA and the Social Security Administration to classify him as 100 percent disabled because of his fraudulent suicide attempts. The original $1,500 he invested in his church mushroomed into a lucrative Merill Lynch portfolio worth $531,700.00 by the time of his 1987 arrest. These resources enabled him to purchase a Rolls Royce, a Dodge, and a 1968 Cadillac Eldorado.

It was while driving the sleek Cadillac Eldorado on Girard Avenue that Heidnik encountered Josefina Rivera.

Heidnik's arrest on March 25, 1987 became national and international news. *The Los Angeles Times* reported on April 3, 1987: "A man charged with murder after police found half-naked women shackled in his basement and body parts in his freezer tried to hang himself in a jail shower during the night."

The story went on to explain how Gary Heidnik "used his T-shirt to hang himself from a shower pipe at the Philadelphia Detention Center," and that the officer assigned "to watch the suspect in the shower temporarily lost sight of him through the steam." His suicide attempt again failed.

While waiting for his preliminary arraignment after his March 1987 arrest, Heidnik was incarcerated at the Police Administration Building. It was there that he was beaten up—his nose broken—by detainees.

What haunts Gallagher to this day is what happened when the first-degree verdict was read in court. It was then, he says, that he began to wonder about the fate of Anjeanette Davidson, the mildly mentally challenged woman Heidnik was living with in West Philadelphia in 1978.

"I believe he killed her," he said. "When they were living together they had a baby [Maxine Davidson] but the baby was taken away from them because neither he nor Anjeanette, who was also mentally challenged, had any prenatal care and didn't go to doctors. After the birth they were told they could not take the baby home with them. But during a trial for his abuse of Alberta, Anjeanette's sister, Anjeanette could not be found. "

Anjeanette, as it turns out, was never found.

After Heidnik's conviction, Gallagher asked the sheriff to ask Heidnik, who was back in the City Hall holding cell, where Anjeanette was.

The sheriff returned to Gallagher with Heidnik's answer: "Fuck you."

While on death row, Heidnik claimed he was innocent of any crime.

"I say real or phony, they can execute me, because I am innocent and I can prove it.... That is the end of capital punishment in this state. When you execute an innocent man, knowingly execute an innocent man, you know there will be no more capital punishment in this state and possibly anywhere else in this country. And you know I didn't kill them two women. Go ahead and execute me.... Yes, I want you to execute an innocent man so there will be no more capital punishment."

So the crazy (but not so crazy) genius-level fraudulent suicide-faker, for once in his life was right.

PHILADELPHIA AND THE 1990s

When Ed Rendell became Philadelphia's new mayor in 1991, one of the first things he did was roll up his sleeves, grab a wash bucket, and head to the men's rooms in City Hall. Local news channels showed clips of the mayor scrubbing the bathroom walls and stall doors clean of graffiti and obscene messages. For a new mayor, this was the perfect photo op, as a clean-up of City Hall bathrooms was a long time coming. Throughout the 1970s and 1980s, dirt, graffiti, and obscene drawings of all kinds covered the walls and stall doors in the City Hall men's rooms.

There was minimal security in City Hall at the time, and anyone could walk in and use the restrooms for whatever purpose they had in mind. One could also tour the building's foreboding-looking but fascinating basement, which I did a number of times (thanks to a friend who worked for the city). What impressed me most about the massive dungeon-basement was its catacomb-like nature and stockpile of old desks, chairs, cabinets, and who knows what else stuffed behind this and that.

ROOM 646 AND ELMO SMITH

When my jury summons notice appeared in the mail, all I could do was breathe a sigh of despair. You know how it is: the jury in-take crowds, the lists of instructions to be followed, the canned videos, and the line formations going to the rooms of the various judges. The last time I received a jury summons was five years ago. Back then my name was called along with other names for a case, but just as our group was about to head to the courtrooms, we were informed that the two parties involved in the case came to a settlement.

Obviously, this was not an exciting criminal case but just another lawsuit. "You can collect your check and go home," we were told.

In prior years, it was my belief that I was never accepted as a juror because I noted on the questionnaire that I was a journalist. I assumed this was the reason because during personal questioning by the attorneys, I felt that the word journalist was a buzz word, a kind of psychic red flag. Since that time, I have been of the opinion that lawyers would rather not have a journalist as a juror. Could it be because they think journalists are going to write about the case or critique their courtroom performance in some way?

My most recent jury summons broke the mold. When I was questioned by a court official and attorneys for both the plaintiff and the defendant, they seemed excited about the "J" word. In fact, the court official immediately began telling me that he has read a number of things I have written over the years. "I know who you are," he said, looking me square in the eye, but with a smile. "I know who you are, Tommy Nickels!"

He was a tall man from South Philly and he very much reminded me of Frank Rizzo. He was almost as tall as Rizzo was, and he even spoke like Rizzo, enough to make me wonder if he had ever known the former mayor.

I did, in fact, ask him that a little later, to which he said: "Yes, I knew Frank. He had an appetite like no other. He once ate three entrees of mussels in front of me, and he devoured three long rolls of bread."

The case I was being auditioned for called for eight jurors out of a pool of thirty people. You can imagine my surprise when my number was called.

"You'll be here till Friday," the court official told us. "That's three days."

Entering and leaving City Hall is much easier as a juror. The procedure is simple: bypass security (always a pleasure), take the elevator to the appropriate floor, then head for your assigned jury room and hang out with the other jurors until the judge calls you into the courtroom.

The general jury selection process, however, is like cattle herding. Years ago, the city provided drinks, soft pretzels, and donuts for all prospective jurors. These were the lush years. At that time, nobody had to stand during the selection process because there were not enough chairs in the main hall, but that is no longer the case. I stood for over an hour in the massive room as various groups were called into different courtrooms. I am not sure why the place was so packed. Are there that many cases being tried in the city of Philadelphia? Even if there are a lot of courtroom cases going on, why book more people than the room can hold?

It was a very hot day when the selection process was going on, so people did not look to be in a very good mood. Having to pass through "take off your belt" security is humiliating enough, but when people discovered that there were no empty seats in the hall, the mood in the room seemed to thicken. It took a court official, the one who calls names and takes attendance, to lighten the atmosphere.

Ms. X worked the room like a high energy stand-up comic, although two hours later you could feel her spirit diminishing. She told jokes and offered antidotes like a cruise ship MC. She would mimic being tough, then giggle and wink at the crowd. At one point, she announced that far too many faces in the room looked depressed. She tried her best to be a mood-altering drug.

Her job was not easy. Sitting there waiting for my name to be called, I realized how many strange names there are in the city of Philadelphia. Names like Philomena Villanova, Myers Pumpernickel, John Peter Savior, and Sayczar Akaka

Apple came rolling off her lips. Ordinary names seemed scarce. This must have been the odd name day. Some names were so weird she had to spell them out because she could not pronounce them.

When she called your name, you had to answer with the word "here," a system that reminded me of my grammar school days when the nuns would take attendance. Everybody had a different way of saying "here." Some people mumbled it, some shouted it, while others seemed to go silent when they heard their name. A woman with short black hair reading a *Harry Potter* book responded with an upright jerk and a loud "yep!" when she heard her name. Several jurors answered with a depressed-sounding "yes" while others, it seems, could barely speak at all. Their voices were so soft most assumed that they had fallen asleep in their chairs.

Standards have gone by the wayside when it comes to how people dress for jury selection. Many were dressed as if they were headed to a summer picnic or ball game—shorts, t-shirts, sandals, and sneakers were not uncommon. Some even wore dirty, stained shorts. One man was in a tank top, his arm tattoos exposed like sun-bleached leper sores. The women were better dressed overall. What these men in shorts did not count on, however, was the fact that once they were pulled into a courtroom—where the air conditioning turned the environment into an Arctic blast—they began to freeze. As in, really freeze.

In fact, everyone who was in extreme summer dress complained of the high air conditioning once they got into the courtroom. "Please turn the air conditioning down," they pleaded.

The attorneys, in full suits and ready to go into slick attorney mode, were comfortable. "Over our dead bodies," they must have wanted to say, but did not. Tank tops may be good on hot days when you have to weed a garden or take out the garbage, but when did they take the place of real shirts?

"Remember people, no open toe shoes or sandals in the courtroom," the court official told our little group of eight. "No flip flops. Flip flops are for the beach, for those zany, Wildwood days, but not court! Dress appropriately, please. Please!"

While going through security on the morning of the first day, I noticed that a guy behind me was dressed in short Bermudas and a tie dye shirt. "You're the first guy I've ever seen wear shorts to a Jury selection session," I told him.

"Well," he said, "I wear a suit every day and when they said we could dress comfortably, I thought of shorts." We laughed at this and went our separate ways, but I could not help but wonder at the word comfortable. One person's comfortable is another's inappropriate attire. Imagine a judge in flip flops and a tight tie-dye shirt tucked into ballet-tight Bermuda shorts. If anybody should be comfortable, it should be a judge.

Yes, it was really good to know that it was the "naked" ones who got their just desserts when they arrived in the sub-freezing courtrooms and begged officials to turn down the air conditioning.

On day two of the trial, our court guide told us that the jury room where we met in the morning and where we took our five- or ten-minute breaks was once a City Hall holding cell. The guide pointed to a row of pay phone shells, where the newly arrested could make their one constitutionally guaranteed phone call. "Elmo Smith was in your holding cell," the official explained. Elmo Smith was arrested and charged with the brutal death and rape of a sixteen-year-old Manayunk resident, Maryann Mitchell. Mitchell, a student at Cecelian Academy, had been out with girlfriends on the night of December 29, 1959 to see the movie *South Pacific*. After the movie and a stop at a hamburger joint, her friends left her at a bus stop so that she could make her way home. Her body was found the following day near Harts Lane in Whitmarsh Township. Like the Center City jogger case at 21st and Pine Streets in Center City in November 1995, the Mitchell case was a gruesome one.

Our guide told us that he had seen the files on the Mitchell case in the City Hall archives. I did not have time to tell him that when I was working on a story about the Center City jogger case, I was shown an upsetting photograph of Kimberly Ernest's body at the base of the stairwell at 21st and Pine. The photo upset me for weeks.

The Maryann Mitchell case rocked Philadelphia like no other murder case in the '50s and '60s. Women everywhere were afraid to go outside or were constantly looking over their shoulders for "another Elmo Smith." Smith, a handyman with a long arrest record for rape and attempted abductions of young females, was the last person to die in Pennsylvania's electric chair.

Of course, there is not much in Jury Room 646 that still resembles a holding cell, although you might make a case for the small caboose-style windows that form the base of a much larger window. There is also an old radiator painted brown or dark green that was undoubtedly in the room when it was a jail cell. Had Elmo Smith ever reclined against the radiator and reviewed the events of December 29? Had he shed a tear? Or did he grip the edges of the radiator in an act of frustration over being caught?

In ways that we cannot fathom, all rooms hold memories. The fears, agony, and pain of people once confined to certain rooms can seep into the walls, forming shadow impressions that a sensitive person can pick up. There have been many rooms in my life that have caused me to say, "Something went on in here."

Around the corner from Jury Room 646 is an old staircase that looks to be falling apart. It is a narrow staircase with tattered paint and split wood; although, you can see that at one time it was a very fine staircase. In some ways it resembles a staircase that was meant to be kept secret, but here it was in full exposure, lonely, decrepit, one of City Hall's secrets. What had happened on those steps? Who was pushed, handcuffed or threatened?

On day three, we deliberated in the jury room, and that is when things got crazy.

When it came time to select a foreman, I was surprised when most of the jurors said they wanted me. But that was no sooner said when the one woman in the room said that the honor should go to the really, really quiet guy in the back who has hardly said anything "since we got here."

Life is strange, and it was too hot to argue. I gave the odd honor to the quiet guy, but soon after regretted giving in so easily.

1

"SOMETHING TERRIBLE HAS HAPPENED IN PHILADELPHIA"

Robert Milton Larsen

The Second Empire row houses built in 1880 in Philadelphia's 21st and Pine neighborhood are made of gray slate and form a distinctive look, at once eye catching and evocative of another era. The historic Edward Drinker Cope House is located here at 2100–2102 Pine Street, the longtime home of Edward Drinker Cope (1840–1897), a prolific geologist and paleontologist who was one of the leading natural scientists of the nineteenth century. Cope's house was declared a National Historic Landmark in 1975.

The Cope house is identical to the other adjoining gray slate homes on the southwest corner of 21st and Pine. These houses form an impressive unit and strike the passerby as uniquely different. The houses are three and one-half stories in height with larger ceilings with a mansard roof at the top floor.

They stand in stark contrast to the houses on the other side of the street which have a traditional town home look. Philadelphia, often called the city of neighborhoods, seems to come together in this part of the city. This neighborhood, which houses small law firms, a super market and several restaurants, is a quiet and residential halfway point between Rittenhouse Square and Fitler Square.

In the early 1900s, Pine Street was cobblestones and a trolley line ran the length of it.

A nearby side street, Taney Street, once led into an Irish neighborhood with its own legendary past—some of that past disordered with shady bars and no-nonsense cliental like the salons in the Old West. In the 1990s, the area was popular with students and city residents who tended to apartment hop. The gray slate houses at 21st and Pine were mainly apartments, while the houses on the other side of the street tended to be single homes.

The area has the distinction of being just far enough away from Center City so as to afford a degree of quiet and a suburban like rhythm. If you are a walker, you will notice that the hubbub and noise of downtown seem to dissipate around 17th and Pine, so by the time you reach 21st you are well out of the noise bubble.

Walking west several blocks on Pine past Taney you come to a small park by the Schuylkill River with a series of pathways, benches, a swing set for children, and a small community garden. Beyond the park, prior to the rehabilitation of the area in the early 2000s, there was an industrial railroad wasteland, owned by Conrail. The tracks were used by slow-moving freight trains that meandered through a series of open warehouses and decaying loading docks. The area formed a kind of lost land where city residents, confined to their apartments or townhouses, would sometimes visit, alone or with their dogs, to escape feelings of urban claustrophobia.

This small industrial wasteland also attracted misfits and vagabonds who hung out in the open warehouses. The homeless also spent time here because in the downtown areas police did not tolerate loiterers. The Conrail police, however, were especially active, and stories circulated that if one was caught walking the tracks near the warehouses—and into the thick and inviting woods that led to the grounds of the Philadelphia Museum of Art—one would be slapped with a trespassing fine.

During the day, the small park—often referred to as Judy Garland Memorial Park because of its attraction as a gay cruising area—was a gathering place for sunbathers, dog lovers, and people sitting on benches reading. Children swung on nearby swing sets as students played Frisbee on the grassy vast stretches of grass.

At night the park was transformed when men came for the cruising and public sex in the darker areas near the fence bordering the tracks. Judy Garland Park was an after-hours destination place. Men lingered and waited while others huddled in circles, all of them on the lookout for the police who made surprise appearances in patrol cars dizzy with flashing lights and orders to "Get out!"

Families, children, and dog walkers avoided the park late at night so there was a degree of indifference from neighbors regarding the goings on there. This changed as public cruising fell out of fashion with the coming of the internet, but sometimes tensions erupted. While Center City residents generally supported "gay rights," the cheering stopped when it came to public sexual displays. Nevertheless, the attraction of the park as a place to get away from congested downtown and as a place to walk "alone" among an interesting industrial setting always remained high.

In 1995, Ed Rendell was mayor of Philadelphia, Bill Clinton was in the White House, and Anne de Harancourt was president and CEO of the Philadelphia Museum of Art. It was a vigorous and exciting time to be a Philadelphian. Homelessness, most notably drug-addicted homeless, had not yet reached epidemic proportions but was still mainly contained in small areas of the city. People who begged in the street were called panhandlers or street people and tended to be older, not men or women in their twenties with a chronic drug problem. In 1995, life was good.

A CRY FOR HELP?

The noise—a chorus of male voices—ran through my head like an exploding bomb. I had been asleep from 11 p.m. the night before but the sound woke me up so abruptly I bolted upright in bed and thought, "What was that?" It was very dark outside; the time sometime near early morning, perhaps close to 5 a.m. The shouts were not an extension of lucid dreaming because my sleep that night was dense. The shock of the noise was so great it woke me up in a panic. It was as if someone had entered the apartment.

The date was November 2, 1995.

The shouts seemed to come from the front of the house, but like claps of thunder they quickly came and went. Drunken Penn students walking underneath my window would not likely scream just once and then go silent. Sitting upright in bed, I listened for aftershocks, conversations, cries for help, but there was nothing.

I went back to sleep. "Nothing," I said to myself, "Just the sounds of the city."

My alarm clock rang not long after this. I shaved, dressed, and went to my little Pullman kitchen and made coffee, lingering by the large kitchen window overlooking 21st and Pine Street as I did most mornings. It was a dreary overcast morning, fairly typical oppressive November weather. Gazing out the window, I saw that Pine Street was full of fallen, wet leaves. It was also intensely quiet, although I knew that within an hour or so that would change when Penn students would begin their walk down Pine on their way to the 34th Street campus.

I thought about the noise I had heard a couple hours before while watching more leaves fall from the trees.

I had come to love this quaint street with its Parisian feel, its quirky neighbors, and live-and-let-live attitude. Around the corner was the Rosenbach Museum and Library that housed a number of famous literary manuscripts, the most famous being James Joyce's *Ulysses*. Across the street from the Rosenbach was novelist Pearl Buck's Philadelphia townhouse (although she was long gone by 1995). The little neighborhood sat between Fitler Square—a picture postcard setting of dainty beauty—and the larger and more vibrant Rittenhouse Square. A rich variety of shops and restaurants gave the area a rich, tidy dynamic, a small town within a larger city.

"Falling leaves are evil," a friend of mine once pontificated. "Leafy pavements are evil." This friend was mostly referring to falling leaves to denote sinister moods in Italian *noir* horror films, especially the films of Dario Argento. If falling leaves were evil, then Pine Street was very evil on the morning of November 2. November, of course, was the month of leaves and gray skies. Soon the cold and snow would come, but November's transitional weather seemed to suggest unwanted surprises.

After breakfast, I left my second-floor apartment and walked down the long flight of stairs past my neighbor Allen's apartment on the first floor. The stench of burnt fish, Allen's favorite dinner dish, filled the foyer of the building as I made my way out the double set of doors to the sidewalk. On the sidewalk, a thought occurred to me to cross over to the other side of the street by the basement stairwell attached to a small law firm. The stairwell was mainly a janitorial breezeway: on trash days, a janitor at the law firm could be seen bringing bags of trash out of the stairwell and placing them on the street.

The bottom of the stairwell was a magnet for fallen leaves and an easy receptacle for litter.

Out on the street, I did not follow my hunch and cross the street where the stairwell was, but continued on my way down my side of Pine, passing the local pizzeria and then heading over to Spruce where my early morning job was located. Had I followed my instincts and crossed Pine, I might have seen a pair of head-phones on the ground, picked them up, and then inadvertently glanced into the stairwell and seen the horror.

The horror at the bottom of the stairwell would soon turn Philadelphia on its head.

Returning from work a short time later, I noticed a neighbor, Mr. Fineman, standing near the stairwell at the corner of 21st Street. Mr. Fineman had been out walking his dog, something he did every morning. I knew him as a nice neighbor who usually said hello to me in the street.

Mr. Fineman seemed to be looking up and down 21st Street as if expecting someone. Mr. Fineman was an illusive character, a widower of advanced age who kept to himself inside his small wooden house that many called the oddest-looking house on Pine. His house was set back from the street and had a porch, an unusual sight in the Rittenhouse Square area.

Mr. Fineman greeted me with his usual "hello" as I walked to the corner of 21st and Pine, adding that he was waiting for the police because there was an injured person at the bottom of the stairwell.

By now, the gray November skies had improved and the early morning chill had dissipated. The sun was beginning to make an appearance.

A barrage of police cars, sirens blaring, then began racing up 21st Street. Mr. Fineman walked to the curb as patrol cars came screeching to a halt. Seconds before the police arrived, I had thought of taking a peek into the stairwell but decided against it. That kind of voyeurism would appear crude, especially if the injured person was awake and conscious. Moments later, I would regret not taking a look.

Mr. Fineman's little dog, hyperventilating and walking in circles, barked as officers and ambulances began to arrive.

The highly dramatic scene was building fast.

Mr. Fineman was questioned by an officer as other officers headed to the stairwell, their gazes fixed for a long time at what they saw.

The person in the stairwell was not a homeless man with a broken leg as I had imagined, but a dead body. Why had Mr. Fineman kept this fact a secret? Is it possible that he really did not know? The sight in the stairwell was obviously very disturbing because the officers looking into it seemed transfixed.

Mr. Fineman's mention of an injured person was a gross understatement. When I viewed a police photograph of the body in the stairwell in 1997, it was even harder to understand why Mr. Fineman thought the person in the stairwell was injured and not dead. The body in the photograph was in a facedown kneeling or crouching position over the last few steps of the stairwell, suggesting that the victim had attempted to crawl up the steps but died in transit. Even a quick look at the victim in this position suggested the frozen-in-motion *tempus frigidus* that most people would associate with corpses.

At this time, 21st and Pine was an official crime scene as officers began arranging yellow tape around the stairwell.

As police marked off the area, I crossed over to my side of the street while detectives and medical personnel converged near the stairwell. A crowd was beginning to form as word spread that a body had been found. News trucks flooded the area and then camera crews began filming the area.

The body—word spread that it was a woman's body and that she had been murdered—was removed from the stairwell but the police tape remained in place for hours. While this was going on, plainclothes detectives in search of clues canvassed the crowd that had converged on the corner. When I volunteered my own story of having heard a loud scream in the wee hours of the morning, a detective informed me that another neighbor had heard a loud noise as well. I was then asked if I wanted to make an official statement at the 24th District; when I agreed, I was driven in a squad car to the District.

Interestingly enough, for some weeks prior to the murder, there had been reports of a "Peeping Tom" in the neighborhood.

The man in question—his identity was never discovered—prowled the neighborhood at night searching for apartments where a young female might be living. The Peeping Tom was obviously just an irascible fellow who did no real harm and he would have gone unmentioned in the press had not a dead body been found in the stairwell.

By early afternoon, there was still a fairly large crowd in front of my apartment building.

Standing there among neighbors and passersby, it was easy to recall the urban myth that had murderers often returning to the scene of the crime. Playing with this gothic notion, I scanned the faces in the crowd. Most were neighbors, just as my neighbor Allen, or Pancake, as some of his friends called him. Allen was never without his baseball hat (mostly to hide his baldness). He was on the sidewalk alone, without his alcoholic young boyfriend.

I did notice an unusual-looking man, a bicycle messenger who could have doubled as a jockey, dressed in dungarees and a plaid hunter's jacket who reminded me of a character out of a Charles Dickens novel. The little man had much to say about his bicycle travels around the neighborhood. The gathering on the sidewalk had turned into a community meeting of sorts with people talking with people they would not normally interact with. For months after the discovery of the body, I had ongoing conversations with the bike messenger who liked telling me what he was seeing and hearing on the street.

By evening, the stairwell was fully decorated with flowers, teddy bears, rosary beads, notes, and votive candles. It had become a small shrine where random people would come by to kneel on the sidewalk, make the sign of cross, and say a prayer. Some people stood in front of the stairwell as if in another world. The flowers, tributes, and stuffed animals would increase in the coming weeks.

The evening news confirmed that the dead person found in the stairwell at 21st and Pine Streets had indeed been murdered.

The victim was identified as a twenty-six-year-old paralegal assistant, Kimberly Ernest, who lived on nearby Spruce Street who had been out on her usual early morning jog when she was killed by an unknown assailant(s).

Ernest's picture appeared on the front page of *The Philadelphia Daily News*, along with a detailed physical description describing her as an athletic women with a shock of strawberry-blonde hair who would jog up and down Pine Street every day in a pair of headphones, the same headphones that were found in a pile of leaves on the sidewalk near the top of the stairwell on the morning of November 2.

The *Philadelphia Daily News* reported that, "In the dead woman's hometown of Hinsdale, Ill., a western suburb of Chicago, a woman who identified herself as Dorothe Ernest, told a reporter, 'I have no comment, please, and I would appreciate it if you don't call back. We need time, please.'"

The *Daily News* also quoted Ernest's boss, Russell Cunningham, at the law firm Larrabee and Cunningham on Walnut Street near 15th Street, where Ernest worked on real estate and tax cases. "She was just a gem of a person," Cunningham said.

The newspaper quoted detectives as saying that Ernest's body "was clad only in Nike sneakers, white socks, a black sports bra, and a ripped black tank top."

After viewing Ernest's photo in the newspaper, I recalled how I had often seen Kimberly Ernest jogging on Pine Street in the late afternoon or early evening. Sometimes she would run past me on the street, dressed in her trademark sleeveless tank top and shorts. What caught my attention was the way her long hair flew out in every direction. From my large kitchen window I would sometimes see her jog past the same stairwell where her body would be discovered.

This caused me to wonder if there was anything inside a person—a premonition—that might cause them to feel something odd when they passed a location where one day something traumatic, like death, would happen to them.

Many city joggers used (and continue to use) Pine Street as their running path to Judy Garland Park. At the park they would circle around and then make their way back, coming and going like this all day long. Pine Street was a jogger's paradise. Friends and I would often marvel or make fun of a new style of jogging then popular called power walking, a cross between a fast walk and a jog which made the jogger look like they were imitating Charlie Chaplin. This style of jogging seemed to be a special running style among women.

Generally, there were few if any joggers on Pine Street between the hours of 5 and 6 a.m., so the presence of Kimberly Ernest at that hour was a rare phenomenon.

The days after the murder passed without any leads in the case, but the shrine in front of the stairwell was now turning into a kind of cathedral. Periodically I would gaze out of my kitchen window and watch as passersby would leave more stuffed animals and notes to Kimberly. Often traffic would slow down near the stairwell and occasionally drivers would get out of their cars and walk over to the shrine.

Once again this made me think of the noise I had heard in the wee hours prior to the discovery of the body. Did I hear a noise related to the killing? It was almost certain that I did.

The break would come a few days after the murder when a career-criminal named Herbert Haak III, at that time in prison because of a parole violation, confessed to his counselor that his friend Richie Wise had killed Kimberly Ernest.

Reporter James Ridgway de Szigethy wrote in his August 2000 article "Mobbed-Up," that Haak's story would change constantly at each retelling. "In some versions he was an accomplice; in others, he played no role at all. The big break in the case came just weeks later, when Haak's own step-father went to the authorities to claim that Haak had confessed to him his role in this sensational murder."

On November 30, 1995, *UPI* reported that two small-time thieves were arraigned on charges of killing a female jogger (Kimberly Ernest) who caught them breaking into a car in downtown Philadelphia. The break in the case was a cause for celebration:

Herbert Haak, 25, and Richard Wise, 19, have confessed to clubbing 26-year-old Kimberly Ernest with a tire jack on Nov. 2, then raping the dying woman, according to police. Police said the suspects admitted they were trying to steal a late-model Plymouth Acclaim at about 6 a.m. when they were approached by Ernest, a paralegal who was taking her regular morning jog. According to the confession, when Ernest threatened to call police, Wise grabbed her. Ernest, who stood 5 feet 10 inches tall and was in excellent physical condition, was overpowering Wise until he smashed her in the head with the car jack. Police said Wise and Haak then dragged Ernest into their car and Wise sexually assaulted and strangled her. The men then drove around for a few minutes before dumping the body in an outdoor stairwell several blocks from where Ernest was killed, police said. Ernest's body, clad in sneakers, socks, a sports bra and a ripped tank top, was discovered about 6:30 a.m. by a man walking his dog. Police said Haak and Wise, who had lengthy criminal records, shared an apartment a few blocks from where the body was found. At the time of his arrest, Haak was in prison, charged with an unrelated crime. Wise's pregnant girlfriend had recently obtained a protection order against Wise, who she claimed has been stalking her.

Kimberly Ernest came from Hinsdale, Ill., a Chicago suburb. The slain jogger came from a prominent family. Her father, Dr. Terry Ernest, was head of the ophthalmology department at the Pritzker School of Medicine, University of Chicago. The report went on to say that both men were held without bail pending a preliminary hearing on December 6.

Readers were informed that Ernest had moved to Philadelphia about three years prior. Dorothe Ernest was quoted as saying that she was not surprised her daughter died trying to prevent a crime.

"That's my daughter," she said. "Kim doesn't turn her back on something that's wrong."

Photographs of the killers were published side-by-side in *The Philadelphia Daily News*. The juxtaposed photograph of the killers resembled an Andy Warhol template. To my horror, I realized that I had met one of the men months ago. Yes, there was no doubt about it, no mistake. The thin blond guy in the photo, Richie Wise, was the same thin blond guy who lashed out at me early one morning on Pine Street as I was returning home from a part-time job.

Wise, just nineteen years old, was walking in the middle of Pine Street in the early morning hours like a cowboy in a *noir* western. He was shirtless and taking long agitated strides when our eyes met. Apparently I had allowed my eyes to linger too long on his naked torso when he turned towards me as if preparing to attack.

Raising a fist, he scowled, "What the fuck are you looking at?"

I wanted to tell him, "You should not be walking around half nude," or, "Pine Street is not a monastery where they practice custody of the eyes," but of course that would have brought him over the edge. The way I looked at Wise was rather casual and innocent, a split-second focus that would not have registered as anything special in the mind of a normal person.

When he started walking towards me, I needed no further proof that he was some kind of a mental case. Still, giving someone like this the "wrong answer" meant that things would get worse, so I said to him, "I'm not looking at anything, just coming home from work." The idea, of course, was not to make an issue out of it. My answer seemed to satisfy him so he continued his walk up Pine, perhaps to 17th or 18th Street where in a few short months he and his chubby cohort, Herbert Carl Haak, would attack and kill Kimberly Ernest because she called them out on breaking into a car.

On November 30, 1995 an AP report in *Deseret News* stated: "Mayor Edward G. Rendell, a hard-nosed former prosecutor, wept over the deep basement stairwell where Kimberly Ernest, 26, was found beaten, raped and strangled Nov. 2. Cabbies and neighbors alike spoke out bitterly, and police began an intense manhunt. A mountain of tips and detectives' round-the-clock work led to the arrests Wednesday of two room-mates who lived in the neighborhood. They were arraigned Thursday on charges of rape and murder."

The report continued:

> The crime scene on a tree-lined street of expensive row homes became a shrine, where friends and strangers left flowers, candles and notes. Hundreds turned out for the victim's memorial service, and the trophy for the women's winner in the Philadelphia Marathon on Nov. 19 was dedicated in Ernest's honor.

While I never spotted Mayor Rendell weeping at the stairwell, the mayor was quite emotional at the memorial service for Kimberly Ernest held at the Friends Meeting House in Society Hall. The standing room only crowd, filled with press and Center City residents, listened as the mayor came close to weeping again as he talked about the senselessness of the killing.

PINE STREET: ANTIQUE SHOPS MEET THE UNDERWORLD

Pine Street in 1995 was a gathering place for street hustlers—most of whom were heterosexual who sold their bodies to gay men for fast cash. They came from Philadelphia neighborhoods like South and Southwest Philadelphia, Fishtown, Port Richmond, Kensington, and Bridesburg, and could be found day or night standing on street corners or sitting on stoops. Some sat atop a small stone wall that bordered a parking lot at 17th and Pine. This was the official hustler block, although one could find stray hustlers near the Tenth Presbyterian Church at 17th and Spruce Street, which had a smaller property wall where the hustlers sometimes congregated.

The hustler activity attracted the attention of police who often patrolled the area and ticketed the men, charging them with obstructing a sidewalk. The reality, of course, was that nobody was really "obstructing a sidewalk." The hustlers always sat on stoops or against a building, leaving plenty of room for pedestrians to pass. Although Richard Wise was not a part of the 17th and Pine Street hustler contingent, later it would be revealed that he knew some of the hustlers who frequented the area. This is ironic considering that Wise seemed to be suffering from a most virulent form of homophobia.

The police patrolled 17th and Pine because of neighbor complaints. Men in cars out "shopping" for hustlers would cruise the area, circling the block multiple times. This often created congestion and large processions of cars circling the block for hours on end, especially on weekend evenings.

The interaction between hustlers and drivers was not always peaceful. A driver might "inspect" a hustler and in so doing say a few words to him but then decide on somebody else and move on. The first hustler, feeling rejected, might then retaliate by chasing the car while shouting obscenities or throwing objects at it. More often than not, the area was peaceful, but when these theatrics occurred neighbors were quick to call police.

Some hustlers did not sit on the wall and wait passively for offers but went into traffic to flag down drivers themselves. This created another kind of mayhem, especially on weekends. Quiet times like weekday mornings or afternoons there were often lone hustlers on the sidewalk waiting to make a match.

The face in *The Daily News* photograph that I studied so earnestly was indeed the same person I had encountered in the summer of 1995, some months before the murder of Kimberly Ernest. Although I escaped the clutches of Wise on that summer morning, things did not go so well for Christopher Beck, aged twenty-seven, on the night of October 30, 1995, a few days before Kimberly's murder.

Beck was returning home from a meeting around 10 p.m. when Wise and Haak approached him and demanded that he hand over the jacket he was wearing. Beck refused to comply. News reports later stated that Beck immediately bolted and took cover in a nearby apartment building when Wise and Haak began chasing him. No doubt Beck felt that Wise was preparing to attack him, as he had almost done with me, and decided to take no chances.

Beck, unfortunately, was the loser in this case. When Wise and Haak caught Beck they beat him on the head with a can of tuna fish, which had fallen out of Beck's shopping bag since he had just come from a local market. The blow to Beck's head was so severe it put a dent in the can.

Just as I readily identified Wise when I saw his picture in the *Daily News*, Beck easily identified Wise and told *The Philadelphia Inquirer*, "He [Wise] had very glassy, dangerous eyes."

The tuna can attack got a lot of coverage in the local press and was labeled a homophobic (or gaybashing) attack. In an AmericanMafia.com feature article "Mobbed-Up?" published in August 2000, James Ridgway de Szigethy wrote:

Just three days before Kimberly's murder, Haak and Wise threatened to kill a young man in a gay bashing assault in the same [21st and Pine] neighborhood where Kimberly would later be killed. Wise, who sports White Supremacist tattoos, and Haak, chased down their victim that night, targeted because of his slight build, and beat him repeatedly with a blunt object. Haak would later claim that he was just there as an observer, while Wise carried out the assault...

Court of Common Pleas Judge Willis W. Berry Jr. convicted Wise of robbery, aggravated assault, and weapons violations in the attack on Beck while the charges against Haak were thrown out.

Partners in crime tend to pin the blame for their most horrendous deeds on their accomplice. Philadelphia Detective Tom Augustine kept this fact in mind when he interrogated Herbert Haak.

"After several hours of interrogation by the skilled and experienced Detective Augustine, the cops had two signed confessions to the murder of Kimberly Ernest," de Szigethy wrote.

Although Haak was not charged in the assault on Beck, both he and Wise were identified as the duo responsible for a long string of attacks on African-Americans and gay men in Center City.

In another gay bashing case, Wise and Haak came upon two gay men kissing in a parked car and proceeded to drag the men out of the car and beat them. The victims in this case did not press charges because they feared that the publicity surrounding the case would out them as gay and hurt their professional chances at work.

2

MEDIA FEEDING FRENZY

In December 1995, both the *Philadelphia Daily News* and *The Philadelphia Inquirer* published stories about Haak and Wise. In a piece entitled "Trial Set in Jogger Slaying," *DN* reporter Dave Racher quoted from Philadelphia city detective Tom Augustine's interrogation of Herbert Haak after Haak's stepfather, John Hall, known as a notorious prison snitch, ratted Haak out for the killing Ernest. Haak retaliated by also implicating Wise in Ernest's death after learning that Wise had attempted to seduce his girlfriend. Typical low-rent soap opera, as they say.

"I just took out the window of a parked car [at 18th and Pine Streets] when the jogger came by," Wise told the police. "I had a crowbar wrapped so you couldn't hear the glass break. We spotted a car around 17th Street below Pine. I got out of the car. Haak was driving." The two had already stolen one car, but Haak told Augustine that Wise wanted to steal another. While Wise was breaking the window, Haak sat in his Bonneville alone:

> I stayed in the car.... I saw a woman run by. I turned around and saw her and Wise arguing, Then I saw Wise hit her with a jack. She had been knocked to the ground and she had gotten up and she pushed Wise. He pushed her against the car, and then he signaled me to come over. So I drove over to them. Wise opened the back door of the car. I thought he was going to get in and we were going to drive away. He pulled her into the car. She wasn't unconscious, but she wasn't fully conscious.

Detective Augustine asked Haak what he was doing when Wise was in the back seat struggling with the girl. Haak answered, "She was trying to reach up front. I was pushing her hands back."

Augustine asked if Wise admitted raping the girl while in the stairwell. Haak replied, "Later on he did."

Wise confessed that Haak kept yelling at him because Wise wanted to rape her in the car but Haak wanted her out of his Bonneville. Wise offered: "We were going to dump her body in Judy Garland Park at 25th and Spruce Streets, but it was too bright, and there were people around."

Wise said that when he was breaking into the car and first saw Ernest, she was running toward the river and told him, "What the hell are you doing? I'm going to call the police."

"She was right in my face," Wise continued. "I hit her on the side of the face with the crowbar, but she didn't go down. She began to fight with me. She was strong. I hit her a couple more times with the bar and she went down. I drug her over to the car and threw her into the backseat. I kept beating her and she kept fighting. I choked her out. And I was pulling off her pants. I was going to fuck her over."

Haak concurred that once Wise threw Ernest in the backseat of his 1987 gold Pontiac Bonneville, Wise "chocked her out and beat her up, just beat her up." Haak says that while she was being beaten, Ernest kept trying to reach up front but that he kept pushing her hands back. "She was just moaning because she was dazed."

Haak told Detective Augustine that "Wise was pissed because we didn't get to steal the car. He added that he [Wise] had already fucked her up and now he was going to fuck her." "I was driving," Haak recalled. So he ripped off her clothes. "Well, I didn't look back but I heard clothes tearing. Then I heard noises, like grunting noises. She was just moaning because she was dazed."

Wise then directed Haak to drive to the outdoor stairwell at 21st and Pine where they lifted the barely conscious Ernest over the railing (a medical examiner's report would later determine that Ernest died in the stairwell).

At the time of the murder, Wise had been living with Haak for two months in a garage at Haak's house at 24th and Spruce Streets.

This was obviously the reason why I had encountered Wise on Pine Street months before the murder. He was walking to Haak's garage, so he must have been in the neighborhood a lot. Haak's face seemed familiar to me but in a different way. It had a frozen quality, fixed somewhere between a frown and a smile but with a sinister sneer that made him look foreboding.

At this time, I was working as a reporter and columnist for a gay and lesbian newsmagazine called *Au Courant*. I covered all sorts of events for the magazine, from life in a Maryland nudist camp to the opening of the Holocaust Museum in Washington, D.C., to interviews with politicians, authors, and celebrities. I also reported on the doings in the neighborhood, and the murder of Kimberly Ernest certainly fit into that category. *Au Courant* editors Colleen and Joe had taken over the reins of the newspaper after the death of its former editor and founder, Frank Broderick, a former staff writer for the *Philadelphia Gay News* (PGN). Broderick left PGN and decided to publish his own newspaper. For several years, I was also a staff writer and columnist for PGN until events led me to *Au Courant*.

Au Courant's offices were near 22nd and Lombard Streets, not far from my apartment at 21st and Pine. I wrote several columns about the Kimberly Ernest murder, mainly detailing what happened on the morning of the murder, including the strange noises I had heard before dawn.

When Wise and Haak were charged with the murder, I did a follow-up column and wrote about my experience with Wise on Pine Street. Colleen, with her "Irish" red hair and Cheshire Cat grin, had a ready sense of humor that significantly lightened the atmosphere in the office. She had a significant talent for knowing what would make a good story. Co-editor Joe was far more remote and circumspect. Word had it that he was a former Catholic seminarian; his "reserve" and laid-back attitude seemed to be the perfect complement to Colleen's personality.

Once Haak and Wise made their respective confessions, Philadelphians now felt they could rest easy and watch justice take its course. The assumption was that both men would be sentenced appropriately. Both men had made what appeared to be honest confessions and had lengthy police records.

In the months before the trial, the makeshift shrine in front of the stairwell had disappeared, although the memory of the murder lingered. From my kitchen window I watched as fewer and fewer people stopped at the stairwell to say a prayer. Little by little, life seemed to be returning to normal. Occasionally, someone might leave a small memento on the stairwell railing, a pink or red bow or plastic rosary beads. Female joggers now regularly ran past the stairwell, although rarely before sunrise as was Kimberly Ernest's habit. The return of women joggers suggested that women in the city refused to hide away in fear. They would not allow Kimberly's grisly murder to intimidate them.

I had hopes of covering the trial of Wise and Haak just as I had covered the trial of the murderers of gay Levittown artist Anthony Milano in Doylestown, Pennsylvania, in 1988. Sitting in a courtroom with a soon-to-be convicted murderer or murderers is not something you soon forget.

Milano was returning home from a Bible study at his church and decided to stop at the Edgley Inn in Tullytown on December 14, 1987 for a sandwich and a beer before heading home. Hanging out in the Inn at that time were Richard Laird and Frank Chester, two tough guys who hated homosexuals. While not every roughneck is inclined to violent homophobia, Chester and Laird were devious and demonic.

The story of Milano's murder is as grisly as the killing of Kimberly Ernest. In the Edgely Inn, Milano wound up conversing with Chester and Laird. Perhaps the Christmas holiday's atmosphere of easy friendliness drew the three together. Reports claim that Laird and Chester conned Milano into buying them drinks, while Laird muttered comments like, "I hate faggots" behind Milano's back. Towards the end of the evening—the trio left after last call when the two men asked Milano to drive them home—Laird and Chester, by now very drunk, slow danced together in the bar but in a mocking way.

The year 1987 was still a sketchy time to be gay and *out* in a small-time tavern far from the city. After last call at the Inn, Chester and Laird left with Milano in Milano's car and drove around for an hour before the two men turned on Milano. Chester and Laird then burnt Milano's car.

The story galvanized Philadelphia's gay community. The brutality of the crime upset people to an extreme degree. I was certainly one of the upset people, having had a similar but much safer experience when, in 1975 at age twenty-four, I headed out from my parents' home in Malvern, Pennsylvania, on a Friday night to a little bar in West Chester. I had recently returned from four years of living in Boston and Boulder, Colorado, and wanted to explore the local scene before moving to Philadelphia.

At the West Chester bar, I ordered a beer and entered into a casual conversation with a man seated next to me. He was a local who looked as though he had never traveled out of the area. In my mind I was still very much in "liberated" Boston-Colorado mode, and let it slip somewhere in our conversation that I was bisexual.

The moment I said the word bisexual I regretted it because the man jerked backwards on his barstool. His body language communicated hostility, so I knew I had to do quick damage control. I reassured him that my real interest was women. But it was too late; he was already off the barstool and in the back of the bar talking to his buddies, a seedy looking roughneck bunch in plaid hunter's jackets.

His buddies walked to where I was seated, forming a semi-circle around me as I continued to sip my beer. A couple of them began making antigay slurs and talked in high-pitched voices while making limp wrist gestures.

I knew I had to leave the bar as quickly as possible, so I took one last sip of my beer then walked out on the sidewalk towards my car. Immediately after leaving I heard the terrifying sound of men running behind me. When I turned around I could see that the entire group was on my tail. I am a good runner, but I was not fast enough to elude them. They tackled me to the pavement on West Chester's Gay Street. They kicked and punched me but then they stopped and miraculously ran away.

No sooner was I on my feet again than a car stopped in the middle of the street. The driver, a potential Good Samaritan, asked if I was okay, but when I told him the reason for the attack, he raised his fist and shouted, "Do you want it again?"

This was the level of homophobia in many places in 1975.

I never did cover the Wise-Haak trial, but I waited with bated breath like most Philadelphians to see what the verdict would be. I certainly regretted not being able to look the killers in the eye as I had done with Laird and Chester in that Doylestown courtroom, watching as they sat stoned face throughout, Laird with a sneer on his face as if he would murder Milano all over again if given the chance.

As the Milano trial progressed, I will never forget how Chester began looking somewhat perturbed and worried—I thought I saw a look of remorse on his slightly pudgy, pockmarked face—but Laird was the image of the devil himself. Worst of all, I observed Milano's parents, Vito and Rose, sitting together looking absolutely heartbroken. I could not imagine what it was that they were feeling having heard the horrid descriptions of how their son was murdered. I spoke to them briefly, aware that my feeble words of sympathy were not offering them much in the way of consolation.

A FALSE CONFESSION?

During this period of nine years from my nineteenth year to my twenty-eighth I went astray and led others astray. I was deceived and deceived others, in varied lustful projects.

Saint Augustine

Almost as soon as the Wise-Haak trial got underway, a terrible shock reverberated throughout the city. Wise and Haak's attorneys made a statement that the initial confessions from both men were not voluntary but forced. Both men, their lawyers said, were forced to sign blank pages after being beaten by Detectives Augustine and William Egenlauf respectively (Detective Augustine only interrogated Haak but was accused by Wise of "kicking him in the ass.") Their confessions were then written in by the police. Complicating the case was the fact that the DNA found inside Kimberly Ernest's body did not match either that of Haak or Wise. The semen found in Ernest's body had been there before the murder, most likely from a consensual lover the night before her fatal jog. There were no signs of a beating, however, on the mug shots of Haak and Wise shortly after their arrest. Neither of them had a scratch on their faces.

Detective Tom Augustine was a 1967 graduate of the Philadelphia Police Academy. As a rookie cop, he was assigned to the Kensington neighborhood near Lehigh Avenue. Augustine was one of the arresting officers in April 1975 when Mrs. Ellen Judge, aged thirty-two, held up the Industrial Valley Bank on the 2600 block of Kensington Avenue for $3,200. His beat also included the area of 6th and Huntingdon, one of the city's busiest corners for what was then termed "dope peddling." Augustine's beat included the area of Ann and Belgrade Street in the city's Port Richmond neighborhood.

On May 20, 1989, the racially motivated murder of Sean Daily at Ann and Belgrade Streets shocked residents, although Augustine was no longer assigned to the area at the time. Sean Daily, aged seventeen, was attacked on May 20, 1989 by a carload of ten Hispanic males who saw him standing on the corner with three friends. The group was out looking for revenge because one of their own had recently been attacked by white youths in Port Richmond. Daily's friends apparently fled the scene when they noticed a car with the youths inside pull up, and forgot about Sean who was in a nearby alley relieving himself. The group beat Daily with baseball bats and then shot him to death.

Detective Augustine's heroic exploits on June 27, 1976 when he successfully restrained the murderer of Lt. Walter Szwajkowski after Szwajkowski attended a Catholic church on Allegheny Avenue for daily Mass, were written up by *Philadelphia Daily News* columnist Jill Porter in June 1993.

On Tuesday, February 6, 1979, the *Philadelphia Daily News* reported:

Police Officer Thomas Augustine said in U.S. District Court here that he and several other officers went to the Harasimowicz home on Belgrade Street near Clearfield in Port Richmond in early June 1976 to answer a complaint of a "demented male."

When they arrived, Augustine said, Leon Harasimowicz's mother, Bronislawa, 72, said her son was in the kitchen.

Augustine said he went into the kitchen and found Harasimowicz holding a kettle containing hot water and some eggs. He said he took the kettle away from Harasimowicz, and he and the other officers then took him to a mental hospital.

Augustine's testimony came during the civil trial of a $1-million lawsuit filed against the city and nine police officers by Mrs. Harasimowicz, who alleges police beat her son to death after he fatally shot a police lieutenant.

Augustine also testified about the shooting incident, which occurred at Belgrade Street and Allegheny Avenue on June 27, 1976, when Lt. Walter Szwajkowski was killed.

Augustine said that when he arrived, several officers already were struggling with Harasimowicz on the ground. As he ran up to the scene, Augustine said, he saw Harasimowicz had a gun in his right hand.

Augustine said he stepped on Harasimowicz's arm and took the gun away from him. Then, he said, he joined efforts to subdue the suspect.

The officers said he hit Harasimowicz "three or four times" around the back of the head and shoulders to try to stop him from fighting.

"He was fighting us all the way," Augustine said. "He was trying to punch me and kick the other officers."

Harasimowicz was handcuffed within a matter of seconds but continued to struggle, Augustine said.

Twice after the handcuffing, Augustine said, he struck Harasimowicz either with his fist or open hand.

Augustine said he felt justified in hitting Harasimowicz because he "wanted to get the man under control and stop what he was doing. He was going to hurt me, the other officers or himself."

Harasimowicz died shortly after 7:30 a.m. His death was attributed to a drug overdose—he reportedly had taken 100 Darvon tablets earlier that day.

In 2004, Augustine was one of the investigating detectives in the Asia Melanie Adams murder in Germantown. Adams' murder came close to generating the same national reaction that Kimberly Ernest's killing did in 1995. By the time of the Adams murder, however, Augustine's career as a city detective had nearly been destroyed by lawyers who came crawling out of the woodwork as a result of the Ernest case.

Augustine's involvement in the Center City jogger case began innocently enough shortly after Haak and Wise were formally charged with murder. "I was working on another case at the time," Augustine told me, "and my partner Tony Tomaino and I had come back to Headquarters after doing something related to the case. We heard a lot of conversation and commotion going on in another room, so it was obvious to us that they were bringing in another case."

At that point, Detective Paul Musi came up to Augustine and Tomaino and asked them what they were doing. "Nothing," Augustine said, "We're getting ready to go home." Musi asked the men if they would do him a favor and drive a man back to Graterford Prison in the Northeast. Augustine recalls that the man was dressed in a tan prison outfit and sneakers.

"A regular guy, kind of tall, the kind of guy who could be anything ... accountant, car mechanic, lawyer," Augustine recalled. After handcuffing the man they walked him to the car for transport. No sooner were all three men in the car than the handcuffed man began to talk. He brought up the jogger case and told Augustine and Tomaino, "I know all about it."

Augustine, barely able to contain his surprise, turned to the man in the back of the car. "Really!"

"It was my stepson and one of his friends that did it," the man, whose name was John Hall, said.

Augustine could not believe what he was hearing. "What are you talking about?" he said, looking the man over.

"My stepson was there. It was Richie Wise who killed her," Hall said, going into great detail, telling the detectives everything he knew about Haak and Wise. In the meantime, Augustine was thinking, "This is crazy" and asked Hall if he could tell Homicide everything he just said. Hall replied, "Oh yeah, I've dealt with Homicide before. I told them everything."

The detectives dropped Hall off at Gratersford and headed back to HQ when Augustine received a page on his pager. The message was blunt and direct: "Call Homicide right away." They found a pay phone and were directed to stop at a residence on Grant Avenue and pick up a woman named Phyllis Hall and bring her to Homicide.

Augustine recalled what happened when he and Tomaino walked up the front steps of the Hall residence and rang the bell. "The door opens right away and out comes a middle aged woman with dark hair. I introduce myself and tell her that I'm there to take her to Homicide. She begins to scream: 'Herbie didn't kill her! Herbie didn't kill her! It was Richie Wise who killed her! I'm scared to death of Richie Wise. Richie Wise is going to kill me.'"

Augustine and Tomaino managed to make it into the woman's living room, at which point they used the woman's phone to call Homicide. Phyllis Chester listened as Augustine told his bosses that "This woman is telling me that her son was not involved in the murder."

The detectives brought Phyllis Hall downtown, but it was not a quiet ride. "In the car Phyllis Hall is running her mouth, saying how her son Herbie introduced her to John Hall after he met him in prison. I didn't know who Herbie Haak was then," Augustine recalled. "Then she begins talking about how she married John Hall."

At Homicide, Augustine introduced Phyllis Hall to Captain Dempsey and Detective Paul Musi. Coincidentally, Herbie Haak was in Homicide at the same time, although he had not yet confessed to the murder. Augustine announced to Captain Dempsey: "His mother gave him up; his stepfather gave him up!" In other words, he confessed.

Augustine went into another room where Herbie Haak was sitting at a small interrogation table. Haak was 5 feet 9 inches and a bit on the chubby side with dark hair and a fair complexion. Born October 6, 1970, he was aged twenty-five, but an older-looking twenty-five. He sometimes went by the name of Robert Haak or Haak II.

"How you doin?" Augustine said to Haak in his down-home Philly accent.

Haak did not have much to say. "Listen," Augustine continued, "We just picked up your Mom. Your Mom's down here. She told me and my partner that you told her that you and Richie Wise picked up the jogger in your car and that Richie was the one that killed her. Listen, man, do yourself a favor, if you have something to say about this, save yourself!"

Haak finally broke down. "I'll tell you what happened," he said. At that point, he was not handcuffed so he could make his statement as Augustine asked Captain Dempsy for a typewriter, and what in police jargon is referred to as the first and second page and the warnings sheets. Augustine gathered some preliminary information and reminded Haak of his Constitutional rights.

"So I sat there, and I'm a pretty good typist you know, and I typed about 15 pages of his statement including a question and answer sheet when you ask questions after the statement is given. I gave Haak the statement to re-read but I can't remember if he made any corrections or not. He signed off on the bottom of each page. At that point I leave the room while Detective Bill Egenlauf is in another room interviewing Richie Wise, who was born on May 19, 1976."

Augustine said at this point he thought he was finished with the case. He was still looking forward to going home, and this was officially Detective Dennis Dusak's case, after all. He was thrown into the mix just to give his fellow detectives a helping hand. Now he could forget about it.

But there was no going home for Augustine when he later went to work for Dusak and inherited the case. That was when he said he began to realize that both Haak and Wise were going around making statements that their original confessions were beaten out of them.

Detective William Egenlauf, who had interviewed Wise, was in Augustine's words "a well dressed, well spoken gentleman as sharp as they come ... you can't find a better interviewer anywhere." Yet in the new statements being released to the press, Wise charged Augustine with "kicking him in the ass," while Herbie Haak went full throttle, accusing Augustine of putting his feet with his shoes on and pressing them into his chest while he was sitting in the chair in the interrogation room. Haak then stated that Augustine smacked him across the face. Haak made these accusations known to the FBI.

"I was told that the FBI wanted to speak to me as regards a criminal complaint against me because Herbie said I had beaten him," Augustine told me from his home in Fort Lauderdale. "But you know, I've been around long enough to make sure that you don't play with the FBI." When Augustine told his sergeant that he wanted to talk to the FBI, the sergeant stepped back with an uncertain look on his face. "Are you sure you want to do that?" he asked. "Are you taking an attorney with you?" Augustine's answer was no. He was heading straight to the FBI building on 7th Street to find out what was going on.

Once at the FBI office, Augustine was interviewed by a black female agent from the Civil Rights Criminal Division.

"I told her my story," he said, "while showing her color photographs of Herbie Haak and Richie Wise. I had a short sleeve shirt on and I made a muscle with my forearm. I have really good arms and I said to her 'If I punched you or smashed you in the face, do you think you'd have a red mark on your face? Do you think if I had my shoes on that I had on all day and night, if I put my shoes up on your shirt, do you think there would be any marks? That shirt that Herbie had on in the photo—that photo was taken immediately after his arrest—do you see any marks on that shirt?'" The agent examined the photo, looked up at Augustine. A moment or two passed. There was silence.

"It's all bullshit. This is what they do. I'll come back anytime you want, I'll answer any question you have," Augustine told the agent. "This is what they do" refers not only to suspects who change their confessions but to an attorney or a group of attorneys behind the scenes who encourage suspects to take this tact.

Augustine would be hit with that unpleasant reality immediately after the local press published a series of disturbing stories about him. The first headline was devastating enough—"Herbie Haak Testifies That Tom Augustine Beat Him"—but the second headline to make the rounds in city newspapers was enough to destroy the career of far more powerful men than Augustine. That headline connected Augustine with a second crime, the beating of five suspects in another case.

The double whammy greeted Augustine as he left the Criminal Justice Center during the trial of Haak and Wise and he noticed lines of reporters standing in lines over a block long. "Every camera in the city was in my face," Augustine recalled. "More cameras than I have ever seen." The scene was a shark-feeding fest, a media hullabaloo, and pointed to a future course of events that would change Augustine's life forever.

The fact is, Augustine had been warned in the courtroom where Haak was to testify that there was a ruckus going on outside the Criminal Justice Center, and that it was about him. "I was told by a couple of sheriffs that we could leave by a separate entrance. And I said, 'I don't run from anyone.' So we went down the elevator and as soon as we got off the elevator I look over at the side window on Callowhill Street [in the Criminal Justice Center] and every camera is pointed at me. We go out the revolving door and Vernon Odom of 6ABC News shoves the microphone in my mouth, in my face.... That was the beginning and the end of Tom Augustine,'" he said.

There is nothing quite as disarming as a well-known local TV newsperson armed with a microphone and a large camera crew headed in your direction. There is little time to think at a time like this: the microphone becomes an assault weapon. The quest for a hot news story trumps civility, even if the story ends up becoming judge and jury in one distasteful wallop, so that all the public sees is a "guilty" verdict.

Some might say that the reporter in this case, Vernon Odom, was only doing his job when he thrust his baton into Augustine's face and declared: "Do you realize you're being sued—were you a part of *this* detective?"

Augustine had immediate help in the form of Detective Paul Musi, who quickly put his hand in front of Odom's microphone in the style of a priest in an old movie raising a crucifix when confronting Dracula.

Augustine's path through the crowd was cleared for a moment, but more trouble lay ahead. That trouble had to do with Augustine's realization that the forces behind the forced confession narrative were two lawyers, Fred Ambrose of City Line Avenue in Bala Cynwyd and Samuel Malet of Haddon Heights, New Jersey.

Bala Cynwyd is a rather innocuous large-scale corporate theme park, more suburban than urban, where Philadelphia ends and Montgomery County begins. Fred Ambrose's office was in one of Bala Cynwyd's boxy office buildings.

> *The pen had been mightier than the sword but then the tongue took over.*
>
> Amit Abraham

"I was all over the TV. I was national news," Augustine tells me.

Augustine went to work to find out who was behind the attack, and once he discovered the names of the two lawyers, he called one of his professional contacts, the chief of police in Pennsauken, who told him to be wary of Sam Malet. "I want you to know what you're dealing with here," the police chief told him. "All Malet does is sue police departments."

"I'm getting more mentally distraught. I'm fucked up," Augustine said about that time.

"I'm dealing with Malet, Fred Ambrose, Herbie Haak, the fact that the DNA found in Kimberly's body didn't match either Haak's or Wise's, and the fact that the guy who's DNA we thought it was [in Kimberely's body] refused to cooperate."

Augustine was referring to the man who was with Kimberly immediately before her death, a consensual lover from her professional world.

CASTING ASPERSIONS

The revelation that the semen found in Ernest's body was neither Haak's nor Wise's cast aspersions on the reputation of the deceased paralegal assistant.

The news media was playing up the concept that Kimberly was a wild thing—a wild thing who hung out in gay bars and who liked the thrill of one night stands. Like many young single people, both gay and straight, who participated in the nightlife circuit of the 1990s (where one night stands were the norm), Ernest was just following the tempo of the times when everyone was "busy."

An attorney I met years after the murder and the trial of Haak and Wise informed me that a close lawyer friend of his happened to be in a bar-restaurant where Ernest happened to be and said "hello" to her, after which Kimberly presented him with a napkin with her name and telephone number on it.

Another source informed me that Kimberly's one-night stands were highly mechanical in nature: invite a man in for drinks (usually wine or beer), get tipsy, go to bed, then kick the man out after sex. This scenario mirrors the life of many gay men living a fast-lane life in the 1990s, but something seen as "radical" for women who were expected to exhibit nurturing qualities (nest building), or at least invite the man to stay for breakfast.

The many lovers angle of the jogger story was played up in a sensationalistic way, reminding me of a heterosexual version of John Rechy's *City of Night*, a novel describing the life of many urban gay men (in this case, Los Angeles) before the 1980s (the age of AIDS), when sexual encounters were accumulated like golden trophies.

Ernest, in behaving like a single man (gay or straight) was really saying: if men could be cavalier in the expression of their sexuality, so could women, or at least those women who have the appetite or zest for life to do so. Moreover, it might be argued how someone with Ernest's athletic abilities would have a strong libido to match. Working your body regularly, tightening and flexing different muscles with daily jogs may in fact cause one to "feel" the body's impulses and desires in a more intense way than somebody who never thinks about their body. It is understandable how a habitual exerciser like Ernest could become the embodiment of Walt Whitman's *The Body Electric*, a super lover of physical sensation—which would of course include romance and making love.

During the time between the murder and the trial of Haak and Wise, I came to know one of Kimberly's lovers, a blond accountant who once worked with Kimberly in Center City.

I met Chuck (not his real name) when he answered a personal ad of mine in a local newspaper. Chuck, who was bisexual, loved quick satisfaction on the fly. A meeting with Chuck meant there was little to no time for talk, a drink. Chuck would often visit me after work and arrive at my apartment still in his white shirt and tie. Chuck always seemed to be in a hurry, just as Kimberly Ernest always seemed to be when I had spotted her jogging past me on Pine Street.

It was eerie having Chuck visit me in my apartment and watch him as he stood at my kitchen window looking out at the stairwell across the street.

For the longest time after the murder, I had no contact with him, but when he finally visited, he confessed that he had been one of Kimberly's lovers. The news shocked me because while he was seeing Kimberly he was also seeing me. Still, I did not get the feeling that Chuck was in love with Kimberly because he said certain things about her that were a little objectifying. Is it a bad thing to be labeled "kinky?" That word was used a lot in the 1990s. It was overblown and overdone, like Rick James' 1981 hit "Super Freak."

My first thought when Chuck started to talk this way was: "Anyone involved with you would have to be that way. Just look at how you behave, Chuck. No social niceties, zero conversation. You storm the apartment and get down to business like a bull in a sex shop."

Chuck, then, was the "Emperor of Kink."

When medical experts talked about the DNA in Kimberly's body not being that of either Wise or Haak, I naturally thought of Chuck. "Chuck, was it you? Were you with Kimberly the night before she was killed?"

Sometime later, Chuck came forward to offer a DNA sample to see if he was Kimberly's last lover. That was when I saw him on TV walking into the testing site. He was dressed in a suit and tie, his standard dress. Tom Augustine told me that Chuck was very cooperative, a decent guy. He did not refuse to give a DNA sample despite the fact that he was married. He did the right thing, kink or no kink. He had character and backbone. He did not hide out like the infamous "Mr. X," Kimberly's last lover. The tests, of course, confirmed that it was not Chuck's DNA in Kimberly's body.

Tom Augustine recalled this time. "Everyone we spoke to were willing to give their DNA, even though these guys were married and said things like, 'I'll give you anything you need even though it's gonna ruin my marriage, it's gonna ruin my life;' only one person refused to talk to us, a Center City man who was one of Kimberly's lovers."

According to Augustine, the man still works in the city—he knows his name and says the man was in Kimberly's immediate professional orbit but would not reveal it.

One of the most difficult things Augustine had to do was contact Kimberly's mother, Dorothe Ernest, in Hinsdale, Illinois. During those conversations with Dorothe, Augustine says they discussed her daughter's reputation, at least how that was being written and talked about in the media. "My talks to her were about Kimberly's reputation regarding sex, but I didn't want to drag Kimberly through the mud. I wanted Mrs. Ernest to know that Kimberly was very *active*."

Mrs. Ernest's reaction to that news was very calm. According to Augustine, she told him, "Well, you know, I'm so glad that she had that experience." This reaction struck Augustine as remarkable. "Mrs. Ernest without a doubt is one of the classiest women that I ever met. She supported her daughter."

3

THE THICKENING OF EVERYTHING

Once I began to write about the case for *Au Courant*, Chuck stopped coming around to visit. The combination of his appearance on local news channels when he went to give a DNA sample and the attention the case was getting in the press may have been too much for him. I was also asking too many questions about the case when we were together.

"Who do you think killed her if those guys (Wise and Haak) didn't?" He never knew what to say when I would ask him this. It would, of course, occur to me occasionally that he might be the killer. He had the physical strength to do it despite his eyeglasses which made him look harmless in a nerdy way. In some ways he fit the picture of a stereotypical accountant: dull blond hair, pale face, a small paunch as if he spent too much time in the office. He also fit the bland description of some murderers who arouse little suspicion because they are able to blend into the scene. By contrast, Haak resembled a line cook or plumber with his unkempt beard and irregularly shaped jug face. His mugshot clearly shows a bitter individual with issues.

Years after the trial when the case was more or less relegated to the annals of memory, I encountered Herbert Haak on the Market Frankford El. He was seated a few seats away but kept a steady stare on me as I tried to process the face: Where had I seen this man before? It took me a few minutes to recall who he was. The memory came back to me like a punch in the gut: It was a slightly older-looking Haak but the jug-like shape of his face and overall scruffiness was recognizable. Although I had never before spoken to him, he seemed to recognize me, perhaps because of my stories in *Au Courant*.

This leads me to John Hall, the tall, skinny man with venal lips and eyeglasses who Augustine says could have played any role in life: a respectable-looking lawyer, accountant, off-duty police officer, evangelical minister. Indeed, when Augustine showed me Hall's photograph when I visited him in Ft. Lauderdale by the Sea for a series of interviews, there seemed nothing sinister about Hall's appearance at all. Here was just another Everyman, a skinny guy with glasses standing next to a red sports car near a house in the country, his right arm placed in a casual manner over the roof of the car.

But just showing me Hall's photograph in an old newspaper article set off a string of reactions in Augustine that caught me by surprise. "Evil, evil, evil, evil!" the former detective said, his voice rising and cresting into a tumult of emotion. "If John Hall tells you something, you are going to believe it," he said. "That's how good of a liar he is."

Known as a jailhouse snitch, during Hall's years in prison for various crimes he acted as a jailhouse lawyer. With his rudimentary knowledge of law and trials, inmates would come to him and pour their souls out to him. "And then," Augustine said, "What he would do is go to the next room and call down to Homicide and give them all the information from the inmates."

When Augustine showed me a photograph of Hall's wife, Phyllis Hall, I experienced a similar reaction. Mrs. Hall is standing on the front porch of her Philadelphia neighborhood row house on a snowy day, her upper body oddly disjointed looking, her head cocked to one side and her left shoulder slightly raised. The overall feeling of crookedness when you look at her matches the disturbing look in her eyes. A perceptive viewer might perceive layers of deception and subterfuge here, as if the woman had been taken over by forces one could hardly describe as "light." The photograph is ample proof that the eyes are the window to the soul.

Augustine's dealings with Phyllis Hall convinced him that she was an equal match for what he describes as the nefariousness of her husband, John.

"We brought Phyllis down with her attorney when we were going to prep her for the trial," he said. Apparently there were problems, or Phyllis was refusing to cooperate, but the situation was getting testy. Augustine told Phyllis that he knew about her lover, "Fresh," a black man living on the margins of society. He also revealed what "Fresh" had told him about Phyllis' crack habit. Augustine's revelation sent Phyllis into shock.

"When John finds out about this—when he finds out you're seeing a black guy from the projects.... I think it's time you start cooperating with us."

Augustine also recalled the time he drove John Hall from Graterford Prison to the DA's office to prep him for his testimony at the February 1997 Haak-Wise trial. At that time, Augustine led Hall into the interview room where there was a table and chairs. The purpose of the meeting, Augustine said, was to talk to Hall about the place of Haak in his life.

"So, I'm talking to Hall and he's telling me about the prison radio that Haak came into the possession of. He says that inside the radio is a set of pearls that Herbert Haak had taken from Kimberly Ernest when she was killed," Augustine said.

Augustine asked Hall how Haak got the pearls into the prison.

"I don't know but he had the pearls," Hall answered. "You take the battery out of the radio and the pearls are in there." Hall explained more details about the pearls when Augustine, out of the blue, invited him to accompany him into the men's room while he brushed his teeth. The nature of detective work both in overtime hours and overlapping shifts meant that the well-prepared detectives had a stash of toothpaste and toothbrush at work.

"In the men's room, John's standing behind me," Augustine told me. "He's got his back to the stall. I've got toothpaste in my mouth and I'm brushing my teeth and look up into the mirror and see Hall a couple of feet behind me and I say to John, 'You're a fucking liar!'"

How did Augustine know that Hall was lying? Detective's instinct?

"Okay, okay," Hall said, "I made that all up. It's a lie."

"You gave us that story and it's a lie," Augustine replied.

"You're not going to tell anybody, are you?" Hall asked.

Augustine then pointed to Assistant DA Judi Rubino and detective Charles Gallagher who were standing nearby and told them that "John Hall is a fucking liar."

Augustine also decided that he could not go into court and cover for Hall. Hall's lie was bigger than Augustine imagined when it was revealed that he made up most of what he said earlier about his stepson's confession.

Philadelphia *City Paper* reporter Howard Altman in his two-part series on the murder of Kimberly Ernest ("The Kimberly Conundrum," January 14, 1999), wrote:

Three weeks after the murder, police arrested Herbet Haak and Richie Wise, two gay-bashing petty criminals who confessed and later recanted, saying they were beaten and forced to sign blank papers.

The cops were unable to find one eyewitness or one shred of physical evidence proving Haak and Wise killed Kimberly Ernest....

On March 17, 1997, after less than three hours of deliberation, a jury found the pair not guilty.

By this time, Augustine's credibility had been shot. As Ridgway de Szigethy wrote in "Mobbed-Up":

> On the day the trial started he [Augustine] was ambushed on the steps outside
> the Courthouse by reporters who had been tipped off as to a lawsuit that had
> been filed by a New Jersey lawyer, Sam Malat, who represented three young
> men who now claimed that they had been beaten a few months earlier in an
> alleged altercation with Detective Augustine. The stunned Detective categorically
> denied the allegations but knew his credibility had been shot, and like the rest
> of Philadelphia, expected the jury verdict that would come down in March of
> 1997, not guilty. A month later, Malat filed a $75 million lawsuit alleging that
> Detective Augustine had also violated Richie Wise's civil rights.

It did not help that the FBI, the Philadelphia DA's Office, and the Philadelphia Police Department were also investigating Augustine. But the worst was yet to come.

Augustine goes over the details for me, his voice shaking as he revealed how, in 2022, he was still recovering from the emotional and professional assault that besieged him on all sides in March 1997.

The assault that "ended" it all for Augustine happened when news broke that private investigators for Richie Wise were circulating a photograph they said that showed Augustine attending the funeral of Philadelphia mobster Anthony Tura.

> Augustine was said to be working with members of the Mafia as well as crooked
> members of the Bureau of Alcohol, Tobacco, and Firearms, the Philadelphia
> Police Department, City Hall, and the District Attorney's office to cover-up the
> facts as to the "real" killer of Kimberly Earnest. That person was said to be John
> Lambert, the son of a politically connected Philadelphia family. [Mobbed-Up]

But Tom Augustine never did attend the funeral of Anthony Tura, and he never worked with members of the Philadelphia mafia.

In November 1999, Augustine received a letter from the U.S. Department of Justice, Civil Rights Division, clearing him of "allegations that he was involved in a criminal violation of civil rights statues regarding the deprivation of the civil rights of Herbert Haak."

"After a careful review of the investigative reports in this matter, and based upon the information currently available to this Department, we have concluded that this matter should be closed and that no further action is warranted," the letter stated.

CHARGES OF FALSE ARREST AND IMPRISONMENT

In June 1998, three years after Kimberly Ernest's murder, Fred J. Ambrose, chief attorney for Ambrose Associates in Bala Cynwyd, who represented Herbert Haak, announced new evidence surrounding the killing of Ernest. Ambrose was also Herbert Haak's attorney in his civil rights suit against the city for false arrest and imprisonment. The year before in April 1997, Sam Malat filed a $75 million lawsuit alleging that Detective Augustine had also violated Richie Wise's civil rights when, as Augustine told me, he was supposed to have kicked Wise in the ass.

An article in *The Philadelphia Daily News* on June 27, 1998, described Ambrose as making "a theatrical appearance in a Criminal Justice Center courtroom just as Judge D. Webster Keogh was about to sentence the alleged 'prime suspect' [Haak] for a probation violation unrelated to the Ernest case." Ambrose told the judge that he had conducted his own eight-month investigation of the case that brought to light the identity of the new suspect.

The suspect was twenty-seven-year-old John Lambert of 15th Street near Jackson, who also had an apartment in Philadelphia's Delancey Place neighborhood.

Lambert's defense attorney, John Griffin, told the DN that Ambrose's charges amounted to "no verification of anything" and categorized them as "a stunt."

John Lambert was also the son of a prominent attorney in the firm of Duane, Morris & Heckscher.

Tall and slender, John Lambert had long hair which reached just below his shoulders that he wore in a long ponytail. He was frequently seen in the area around Pine and Spruce Streets, especially 17th and 13th Streets where he frequented the gay bars there. Lambert's physical look and behavior recalled an earlier era in America: the peace and love generation around the time of Woodstock.

Lambert tended to be soft spoken and reflective. He carried himself with a calm assuredness which belied his association with the 17th Street crowd of bellicose hustlers. I would often see him walking up and down Pine Street but never stopped to speak with him until a friend of mine—fascinated, I suppose, with his tallness and the pony tail—engaged him in conversation near the University of the Arts.

My boyfriend, Stuart, was an amateur photographer and asked John Lambert if he would be interested in posing for a series of photographs. Stuart occasionally approached men in the street that he found fascinating and asked them the same question. Usually he conducted his photography hobby in his suburban home, but when he met Lambert, he used my Pine Street apartment as a makeshift "studio," something he had done only a few times previously. Stuart also paid the men generously for these photo sessions, since he was largely supported by his wealthy family.

John Lambert was quick to agree to the arrangement.

We invited Lambert back to 2110 Pine to chat, and to make arrangements for the photo session, we agreed would occur the following weekend. In his conversation with us, Lambert was much like the initial impression I had of him: he was a person of few words, a taciturn soft-spoken guy with the "soul" of an old hippie.

Lambert told us very little about his life, mentioning that he grew up in the suburbs, that his father was an attorney in the city and that he had a sister.

Stuart handed Lambert a wad of cash for his time and left the apartment. As Lambert was leaving, Stuart watched him exit the building from my kitchen window.

Stuart was checking to see that Lambert had not stolen anything in the foyer of the building. Stuart's paranoia regarding this was caused by an incident several months prior when, after a photo session with another man, Stuart saw that the man had stolen a massive nineteenth-century wall tapestry of the Nativity that hung in the foyer of the building. The man had the tapestry rolled up like a scroll and ran with it under his arm down Pine towards 20th Street.

Stuart bolted from the apartment, skipping steps as he ran down the long staircase to the street, and made chase down Pine. This was Stuart's way: bold and fearless to a fault. Not more than fifteen minutes later he returned with the tapestry and together we hung it back on the foyer wall in its rightful place.

The following weekend, John Lambert joined us at 2110 Pine where Stuart took a series of photos. These were not images in the style of Robert Mapplethorpe, although they were images that highlighted John Lambert's physique and good looks. One fact came out during this photo session, and that was that John Lambert had a serious heroin problem. This issue was not evident to us before.

After that, Stuart and I would often see John on the street. He was often alone or sitting on a stoop near 15th and Pine. There were also occasions during the week when I would encounter John Lambert during my travels around Center City. Occasionally he would ask if he could accompany me home. When that happened I would often invite him up to the apartment and spend an hour or two with him.

After Ambrose's disclosure that John Lambert was the new suspect in the Ernest murder case, other facts began to emerge.

On the day after Richie Wise's arrest for the murder of Ernest, Wise's father, Leonard Wise, claimed that a former employee of his, Billy Liberatore, had told him that his roommate, John Lambert, killed Kimberly Ernest while high on crack.

Billy Liberatore was a crack-addicted hustler who hung out at 15th and Pine who could often be found running in and out of traffic and stopping cars in order to attract clients.

Liberatore was so careless in his pursuit of men that sometimes it seemed that he was on a suicide mission, approaching anyone he encountered without taking time to discern whether or not they were interested. Underneath the bruises and cuts on his face from his many bullying and adverse street encounters—both with clients and other street hustlers—one could see the remnants of a nice-looking Italian guy. Liberatore's thin build and small frame, as well as a certain feminine quality to his face, suggested the extreme opposite of a violent thug: he was instead a dangerous child capable of any wildcard behavior.

I would often encounter Liberatore during my walks on Pine Street. He would ask for spare change, inquire if I had seen "so and so," or where I was going and what I was doing, and would I mind if he tagged along?

Liberatore's desperation to be "taken in" was legendary. He was in many ways Pine Street's "rug rat," appearing out of nowhere during the day or in the middle of the night and often looking half dead or so stoned he could barely walk. Liberatore was also an incessant talker; words came out of his mouth as fast as he ran across the street to chase down cars. The times when he was not on the street he was in jail.

He was labeled a "crazy" even among the hardcore hustlers at 15th and Pine. Crack had skewed his take on the world, his memory, and the way he related to people.

As a former employee of Leonard Wise, and as John Lambert's roommate, Liberatore told Leonard Wise that John Lambert killed the jogger when he was high on crack. He explained that this was so because when Lambert returned to their apartment there was blood on his clothes. All of this was music to Leonard Wise's ears because it gave him an opportunity to prove his son's innocence. The senior Wise wasted no time tracking down an attorney.

THE ATTORNEY

A good lawyer is a bad Christian.
John Lothrop Motley

A countryman between two lawyers is like a fish between two cats.
Benjamin Franklin

Fred Ambrose of Bala Cynwyd employed a posy of private investigators.

Private investigators are an odd lot. They are not police officers or detectives but sort of freelance vigilante wannabe cops. Like power-hungry security guards who want more power than they have, it can be easy for some PIs to act as if they have legal authority.

One of Ambrose's men, Stephen Stouffer, reportedly claimed to have worked for the FBI and for William Acosta, a former NYPD member. By the time of the jogger trial in 1997, Ambrose's team, which also included PI Skip Thomas, had pretty much packaged the claim that John Lambert was a serial killer responsible for the murders of at least six women in the Philadelphia area. Complicating the scenario, Ambrose's team claimed that Kimberly Ernest was involved with Lambert in the abuse of drugs.

The close-knit gay bar world of Locust and Spruce Street in the so-called Gayborhood was its own bubble universe where everybody "knew" everybody if only by sight as frequenters of this bar or that. Since both John Lambert and Kimberly Ernest had a pronounced "stand out" presence—John with his tall physique and long pony tail, and Kimberly with her shock of ginger hair and Nicole Kidman good looks—they would have been remembered as being among the cast of characters in that area.

In June 1998, *The Daily News* announced that there was a new suspect in the jogger case.

A lawyer who is suing the city for false arrest on behalf of one of the defendants acquitted in the murder of jogger Kimberly Ernest said yesterday that he has identified a "prime suspect" in the case.

Fred J. Ambrose, who represents Herbert Haak, made his announcement in a theatrical appearance in a Criminal Justice Center courtroom just as Judge D. Webster Keogh was about to sentence the alleged "prime suspect" for a probation violation unrelated to the Ernest case.

Ambrose said he came to court to offer evidence that he said the judge should know about his alleged suspect. Speaking in court, he said his own eight-month investigation of the case brought to light the identity of the "suspect." But after leaving the courtroom, Ambrose refused to repeat his accusation.

Under examination by defense attorney John Griffin, Ambrose testified that no state or federal officials had told him that they considered the man he identified to be a suspect. Ambrose said he had his "own criminal and confidential informants," whom he refused to name. He denied that he had anonymously faxed a three-page document to the judge that tried to link Griffin's client to the 1995 Ernest murder.

Griffin told reporters that his client has never been questioned about the murder by police, and he characterized Ambrose's accusation as "absurd." His client was identified in court as John Lambert, 27, of 15th Street near Jackson.

Griffin also dismissed Ambrose's accusation as a "stunt" designed to call attention to the suit he has filed for Haak, who, along with Richard Wise, was found not guilty of the murder.

Assistant District Attorney Theresa Krause, the prosecutor in Lambert's case, told Keogh the government "has no verification of anything" Ambrose said.

Law enforcement sources consistently have said they believe that Haak and Wise, not anyone else, killed Ernest.

In August 1998, *Au Courant* arranged for me to interview Fred Ambrose at his Bala Cynwyd office. The bus ride to City Line Avenue from City Hall to where Ambrose's offices were located is not a long one. The bus briefly travels along the Schuylkill Expressway, passing the Philadelphia Museum of Art and the old Fairmount Water Works which used to house the city's aquarium. Below the Water Works is Schuylkill Falls which frames the Greco-Roman columned portico of the Water Works. As a boy when taken there by my great aunt, I would watch as city kids fished for catfish, some with poles but most with buckets on long ropes that they would lower into the water and then pull up to see if anything was inside. The number of catfish in the river at that juncture was always high, so one could be certain that at least after several tries, there would be an ugly bewhiskered catfish thrashing around inside the bucket.

Navigating the maze of uninspiring office buildings in Bala Cynwyd's corporate center is not easy since everything looks pretty much the same. When I finally located Ambrose's office, I was struck at how small it was. It did not have the space or the personnel of most law firms but seemed more like the congested office of someone starting out on their own for the first time.

Ambrose greeted me cordially, shook my hand, and offered me a seat. I was struck by his owl-like face and somewhat outdated large aviator glasses. Two men appeared out of another room; PI Stephen Stouffer and Ambrose's paralegal/ investigator, Skip Thomas. There was a cursory introduction as the men continued to shuffle about the room. I sensed a heavy, somewhat guarded presence on their end and remember thinking to myself, "There's something really different about this law firm."

Stouffer and Thomas, when they were not moving about the office, sat alongside me so that it felt like I was encased in a semi-circle with Ambrose at the head.

Ambrose wasted no time but went straight into what he thought happened on November 2, 1995.

THE AMBROSIAN NARRATIVE

Ambrose said that when Kimberly Ernest left on her daily jog in the early morning hours, she ran into John Lambert at 15th or 17th and Pine Streets. Watching from the sidelines was a friend of Lambert's, Billy Liberatore.

"Lambert and Liberatore were buddies for a time and often hung out together near 17th and Pine," he said. Ambrose then pointed to Stouffer and Thomas and said that according to their investigation, a statement was made by Liberatore that he was with Lambert on the morning of November 2, 1995 when Kimberly was murdered. Liberatore said that Ernest and Lambert got into an altercation of some kind at 17th and Pine at about 5:45 a.m. in which there was some pushing and shoving. Loud words were exchanged.

"It's our speculation," said Ambrose, "that Lambert continued this encounter with her from 17th and Pine to the 21st Street area—either continued it or again encountered her down at 21st Street. And that led to what happened to her."

Ambrose said he had other (unnamed) witnesses who saw or heard the encounter between Lambert and Ernest on the morning of November 2, as well as other pieces of evidence linking Lambert with the killing, which he was not yet able to divulge.

Ambrose mentioned a police report that had a truck driver spotting Ernest jogging near the intersection of 21st and Pine around 6:10 a.m. At that point Ernest was headed down towards the river on the north side of the street.

KILLER LAY IN WAIT

Ambrose claimed that more than likely Ernest was attacked on her way back from the river while jogging past Van Pelt Street, a tiny street in the middle of the block that runs through to Lombard.

"We think this is the way it was because under Kimberly's fingernails there were traces of shrubbery only found on Van Pelt Street and not on Pine Street," Skip Thomas offered. "There were also hand prints found all over the hood of a neighbor's car, indicating a prolonged struggle. Of course, it is possible that she was attacked on the on the north side of the street on her way to the river, but we don't think so."

If Ernest was attacked on the north side of the street that would place the attack seconds after the truck driver spotted her at 6:10 a.m. Whatever direction Kimberly was going, Ambrose and his team of Skip Thomas and Stephen Stouffer said they were certain of one thing: that the killer was not Richard Wise or Herbert Haak but John Lambert, the guy with the long ponytail.

By the time of my interview with Ambrose, Haak and Wise were both found not guilty in the killing of Ernest. Ambrose at the time was deep into representing Haak with his civil suit against the police for false arrest and imprisonment.

The Philadelphia Inquirer in a March 16, 1997 article quoted jury foreman Paul Hooks, Sr. as saying, "The blood didn't match. The hair didn't match. The semen didn't match. The prosecution never came out with the murder instrument.... There just wasn't enough evidence to put those guys away."

4

WHO WAS KIMBERLY'S LAST DATE?

In Ambrose's Van Pelt Street scenario, Lambert was hiding in the small street until Ernest jogged past. Other probable hiding places include the stairwell itself or a nearby open apartment doorway, which would have made it easy for the killer to dash out onto the sidewalk the minute Ernest was spotted. In the Ambrose version the killer provoked a violent struggle that ended in the stairwell where Ernest was sexually molested and killed.

"The fact that she was sexually molested by her attacker is a given fact at this point. The jury decided this," Ambrose told me. "The semen found in her was left there by the attackers. The DNA did not match Haak or Wise."

What about the DNA from Mr. X, Kimberly's last date?

The stale *versus* fresh semen debate was a sore spot during the trial. For a time the press was reporting that the semen found in Ernest's body was the result of consensual sex some twenty-four hours before—this despite the opinion of the original coroner in the case, Dr. Bennett G. Preston, who maintained that it was not stale sperm and so had to be from one of the attackers.

Ambrose said that during the trial Assistant DA Judi Rubino "acted like she was surprised at the testing ... later on in the case she shopped around for another coroner and he tried to present testing that it was from consensual sex the night before." Fresh sperm won out in the end, which seems to place the killing and the sexual molestation as having happened in the stairwell or slightly before.

If the so called "fresh sperm" was not from either Haak or Wise, was it from John Lambert? And if it was not Lambert's, was it Chuck's, the truck driver who spotted Kimberly jogging, or even the bike messenger I befriended?

When I was brought in for questioning on the day of the murder, I came forward with my knowledge of a neighborhood "Peeping Tom" which I thought may be relevant (as it turns out, it was not.)

At the time I was questioned, detectives were convinced that both the killing and the sexual molestation had taken place in the stairwell, judging by the positioning of the body (an obscene doggie-style position) and the nature of the gashes on and around the victim's head. The detective questioning me then said that Ernest's head had been bashed against the brick wall of the stairwell.

WHY WERE HEADPHONES IN THE LEAVES?

When Ambrose showed me the crime scene photos, I concluded that the positioning of the body indicated that it had either been arranged (and was not merely dumped over the stairwell to fall any which way), or in her last moments of life Kimberly had attempted to crawl up the steps of the stairwell on her knees.

One thing that also struck me was a photograph of headphones in the leaves not far from the stairwell, headphones which Ernest was wearing at the time of her death, and most likely the same headphones I had seen Kimberly Ernest wearing when she would jog past me on Pine Street from time to time.

At the time of my talk with Ambrose, I believed that the headphones in the leaves seemed to indicate that she was probably attacked somewhere on 21st and Pine and not dumped there. An outright attack at 21st and Pine would explain the horrific, piercing screams I heard in the wee hours of November 2, unless, of course, Kimberly regained consciousness at 21st and Pine from the blackjack assault a few blocks away, and fought Haak and Wise who were trying to throw her over the stairwell.

In my article for *Au Courant*, I stated that I believed that the headphones would have "disengaged" in the event of a sudden jolt or attack. If Ernest had been killed in an automobile, it is unlikely but possible that the headphones would have remained in place and then fallen off the body as it was being dumped without the killers being aware of it.

"Look," says Ambrose, "I represent Herbert Haak, and we filed a civil rights case for him last year in federal court. Richard Wise has his own counsel. Basically, for many months now I've been more interested in solving the killing and showing what really happened here, and from what we found out, I'm convinced that John Lambert is the killer and that he did this crime. We basically proved that John

Lambert did commit this crime and right now we're trying to gather evidence that will be admissible in municipal court."

Ambrose was adamant that something went amiss in the original investigation.

"You know," he told me, "It was more than two young men accused with insufficient evidence. From November 2 to mid-November the investigation was going somewhat like a normal investigation would go. Then things started to happen—in my opinion, derailed. My opinion is that Haak and Wise were framed with a combination of coercion and fabrication."

Ambrose's attempt to review the case, the investigation, and other suspects led him to John Lambert. "Talking to various people who say they all remember on various occasions is like a billion little pieces of information that when you put them together they form a picture. Two or three months into our investigation it led very quickly to John Lambert."

Ambrose mentioned Ernest's aunt, Saundra Brewer, who at the time was assistant DA of the city of Los Angeles, who came forward to cooperate with his team. "She has been cooperating with us in giving background information on Kimberly and is reacting the way you'd expect anyone to react to these raised questions."

Sitting there with Ambrose, I was taken with the fluidity of his talk and his reasoning and was beginning to doubt the Haak and Wise narrative.

Turning semi-circle in his swivel chair surrounded by books and files, he would pull out a paper or envelope from this stash and read me something, then swivel in the other direction and pull out another paper. In Ambrose's view, the city's response to reopen the case meant two things. "If they reopen the case, they are going to raise doubts … which raises serious questions about police misconduct," he said. "Any criminal investigator will tell you that … if they reopen the case, they are saying 'Well, there's still a killer out there.' So far their position is, they got the killers, Haak and Wise, but the jury let them off. If they reopen the case they are backing off from that position. I mean, why reopen the case when you believe you have the killer?"

Listening to Ambrose, it occurred to me that that both he and Haak would benefit from the case being reopened. But even if the case were reopened, it would have as many twists and turns as the old one in which Wise and Haak were arrested, tried, and then acquitted.

Skip Thomas, who had been listening quietly on the sidelines, informed me that John Lambert's friend, Billy Liberatore, followed Lambert to the vicinity of 21st and Pine. "We have a statement from Liberatore that he was with Lambert on the morning on November 2 and that when he was in the area of 21st and Pine he saw two people standing in their apartment windows, but he left because he got scared."

It was difficult to imagine Liberatore giving a serious, fact-based statement to Ambrose and Thomas. How did Ambrose's team even manage to get Liberatore to talk in coherent sentences? There was also the question of locating Liberatore to include him in their legal counsel since his movements on the street were erratic and unpredictable. Liberatore seemed mostly indifferent to the dangers in the city—proof of this was the way he would run in and out of traffic stopping cars and flagging down random drivers. Billy Liberatore scared? That did not feel right to me.

When Thomas mentioned two people standing by their apartment windows, he was inferring that one of the people was me. He would not tell me who the other person was. He merely said, "A neighbor." Why the mystery?

Once again, I enumerated for Ambrose and Thomas how on the morning of November 2, I was up at 6 a.m. brewing a pot of coffee in my Pullman kitchen and standing close to my large kitchen window. On that morning I saw nothing. It was damp, overcast, and a little darker than usual in the rainy pre-dawn hours before the body was discovered by Mr. Fineman walking his dog at 7:40 a.m. I reiterated that the only thing I remember seeing that morning when I glanced out my window were a lot of leaves on the street—fallen leaves, a symbol of death, decay, and (in a *noir* film sense) something approaching evil.

I had no way of knowing that Billy Liberatore was glancing up at me from behind a parked car, or even if he was there at all.

I knew that Liberator knew where I lived because sometimes he was in the area around 21st and Pine and saw me enter and leave 2110. Yet it was hard to imagine him involved in a calculated murder and keeping watch, protecting John Lambert, as Thomas and Ambrose inferred, while Lambert murdered the jogger. The scenario as offered by the team felt ludicrous, and yet anything was possible.

Once again I repeated how I had heard a chorus of voices sometime in the wee hours of the morning, before my alarm clock rang at 5:45 a.m.

I repeated the mantra that it was a series of very sharp yells that jolted me awake from a sound sleep, enough to make me sit up in bed and wonder: "What was that?" Since I heard no follow-up screams or police sirens, I went back to bed, assuming it was students on a drinking spree. On the day of the murder, I said how I told police about these screams but they did not seem all that interested.

Then Thomas told me that several other people had heard the screams.

Why was I just now hearing about this? The police officer I spoke to on November 2 near my apartment vaguely alluded to somebody else hearing an early morning noise, but his attitude was dismissive. Thomas gave it much more importance which made me respect what the Ambrose team was trying to do.

But who were these other neighbors, and why were they not quoted in the press after coming forward in a direct way the way that I did? The bigger question was why did someone not call the police after hearing the noise? Did the other witnesses go back to bed just as I had done? And why had a single neighbor not seen anything? Hundreds of apartment windows faced the stairwell and yet not one person saw anything but they heard screams.

"Witnesses in the area," Thomas repeated, "say it is very definite that they heard a screaming female voice in the wee hours of November 2. Some witnesses say they heard a couple of voices but within that chorus they say *they heard a female voice*."

Thomas pinpointed the screaming as happening close to 5 a.m. or a few minutes after. "It's hard to tell," he said. "Everybody's time is different. Nobody's time is the same." He attributed the time variations to "sleep disorientation."

October 29, 1995 at 2 a.m. was also the start of Daylight Savings Time. November 2 was just four days into later sunrises.

Since no automobile accidents or any other incidents at 21st and Pine were recorded as happening in the early morning hours of November 2, Ambrose and Thomas said they were convinced that the screams had something to do with the killing. I certainly did not need Ambrose and Thomas to tell me this.

The interview took a slight turn when Ambrose wanted to know everything I knew about John Lambert.

The question about Lambert was more than a general question but in fact felt much more serious from my point of view, especially when he had me repeat my answers before asking me very pointed questions about my relationship with Lambert. Through it all I had a sense that he was setting the stage for some something far more complicated regarding Lambert that he would revisit later.

I told Ambrose that I saw and spoke to Lambert both before and after the killing of Ernest.

"He was always hanging around 17th and Pine, an area that I pass a lot because it's on my path to work and I have friends in the area," I said. "I'd see John mostly in the early morning hours when I'd be in the area anywhere from 6:45 to 7 a.m. while going to work. John seemed outgoing and friendly and we occasionally had a brief conversation."

I did not divulge any soap opera details, such as Stuart photographing Lambert in my apartment but kept the information general. I left Ambrose's office feeling pretty confused.

Until my visit, I was convinced that Richie Wise and Herbert Haak had killed Kimberly Ernest, but now I was not so sure. I kept thinking of John Lambert as the possible murderer in terms of his intimidating size, his big hands and feet, and how he towered over me (and I am tall by average standards) when he would visit me in 2110.

Ambrose mentioned that John Lambert had a violent streak. He may look calm but when that temper is unleashed he can do real damage, Ambrose noted, citing the time that Lambert allegedly attacked his sister, nearly giving her a brain hemorrhage.

How had Ambrose come upon this information?

On the bus on the way home, I imagined the murder of Kimberly Ernest according to Fred Ambrose: Lambert and Liberatore by the stairwell in the pre-dawn hours of November 2, Lambert having dragged or carried Ernest into the stairwell where he killed her before raping her while Liberatore stood guard, looking for oncoming traffic or pre-dawn risers in the apartments across the street.

It was a believable story, just as believable as Kimberly Ernest interrupting a carjacking while on her morning jog.

I promised myself that the next time I ran into Lambert I would look at him through the lens that Ambrose was presenting, but as it happened there would be no next time. Lambert was already in jail for a drug violation and I would never see him again.

5

A SITCOM STARRING MARLO THOMAS

While working on the Ambrose interview for *Au Courant*, I felt a sense of regret at not picking Lambert's brain or asking him in-depth questions about Kimberly when he was in my apartment.

When I called Geri O' Donnell of the DA's press office to check if she knew anything about a new suspect in the case, she said she knew nothing. On the other hand, Captain Brady of Homicide voiced "no comment" on Ambrose's upcoming press conference to announce the name of the new suspect. "This is a civil matter," he told me, "so in a way I think that speaks for itself. Because it's a civil matter, it's inappropriate for me to comment on it."

So I put a call through to Assistant DA Judi Rubino, but that call went unanswered.

Ambrose, however, told me that he was no longer approaching the case as a civil litigator representing civil rights. "I'm interested in knowing what really happened here," he said. "This girl is dead. She was brutally killed. And the people who did this should be brought to justice."

My editor at *Au Courant* thought it best to scratch John Lambert's name from the piece and instead insert "John Doe" because Ambrose had not yet given his press conference.

I was disappointed because this took the "breaking news" sting out of the piece but later, on reflection, I came to understand her decision. What if, lawyers being lawyers, or Ambrose being Ambrose, the team in Bala Cynwyd suddenly switched suspects and focused on Billy Liberatore as the real killer?

Given the serpentine twists and turns in the case, a last-minute change like this was not hard to imagine. Unfortunately, by the time my interview was published, Ambrose had already given his press conference and John Lambert's name was all over the city. The "John Doe" in my piece felt ridiculous.

The announcement that John Lambert was the suspected killer of Ernest pushed Richie Wise and Herbert Haak further into the background. Wise at the time was in jail for a number of other convictions while Haak would soon be sentenced for check forgery.

Shortly after Ambrose's press conference, Ambrose's office called and requested that I revisit the offices in Bala Cynwyd. Now that Lambert's name was made public, his team was on a roll. Ambrose couched his request for a visit by promising to tell me "something breaking in the case," and so I complied.

When I entered the office both Stouffer and Thomas were present. Ambrose seemed much more relaxed as if he had the world by the tail. We exchanged banal pleasantries, but the whole time I felt that a shoe was about to drop. This feeling was confirmed when, instead of revealing new facts about the case, Ambrose honed in on my relationship with John Lambert.

Previously, I had casually mentioned to Ambrose that Lambert and I had had a brief chat near the stairwell at 21st and Pine Streets after Lambert visited me at 2110 Pine Street. Ambrose would question me about that conversation later, but for now he wanted to know about my meetings with John.

"It was a superficial acquaintance," I told him. "My contacts with him lasted anywhere from a half hour to 40 minutes … very, very light. Maybe three times I had a real one-on-one talk with him."

Once again I avoided telling him and his team about Stuart and the photography sessions. Frankly, I was embarrassed and felt some shame about that, since John was known as a male prostitute and Stuart had paid for his services above and beyond the photo shoot. It seemed to me that Ambrose had already assumed that my connection with Lambert had a gay subtext. The fact that he never mentioned this connection or asked me outright about a possible sexual connection with Lambert struck me as curious.

"So, it was just a social or sort of casual relationship?"

"Yes, yes."

"Did he ever mention Kimberly to you before November of 1995?"

"He never mentioned Kimberly. Certainly if he had said something like he was a friend of Kimberly's or was her boyfriend … that I would have remembered. "

Ambrose removed his glasses and put one of the handle frames in his mouth. "The way that your apartment is set up … apparently your kitchen window overlooks the street and the stairwell?"

"It's about the best view of the stairwell that you can get on that street."

"You are close to Van Pelt Street on your side of Pine, right?

"I wouldn't say it is all that close but it's more like a half block down the street."

"Skip and Steve were telling me that you remember seeing certain things or maybe even saw Billy Libratore or John outside that morning or on the street at 21st and Pine somewhere…"

I had never said such a thing and thought it odd that the investigators would say such a thing. "No, not that morning, no," I replied. "I saw John around the time of the killing maybe weeks after but on that day I didn't see anybody except Mr. Fineman who was outside walking his dog."

Ambrose put his glasses back on. "For many months now I've been re-investigating the murder myself, and I've gotten to the point where I'm more interested in solving the murder and showing you what really happened here. I'm convinced that John Lambert is the killer. He committed the crime."

"You didn't know that you were going to stumble on this evidence when you started out?" I asked.

"It started out as a normal civil rights case and then like any case we have lawyers investigate it, and see what they're doing with it. And very quickly I started to realize that there was something amiss here. It was more than two young men accused with insufficient evidence. It went way beyond that and we quickly found out that these boys didn't commit the crime. And then it led to our investigation with Mr. Lambert."

The way that Ambrose said "these boys" made it seem like Haak and Wise were hooligan delinquents out of an *Our Gang* comedy. I asked Ambrose how he decided that John Lambert was the killer. Why John Lambert and not any of the other miscreants who inhabited the 17th and Pine Street area?

"Well, there are two men there such as yourself talking to various people who knew Lambert, who saw him on various occasions and it was like a million little pieces of information and when you put them together they form a picture. I'd say maybe two, three months into our investigation it led very quickly to Mr. Lambert. That's how we arrived at the point we are at today," Ambrose said. "I don't know if you know John is in jail today," he added.

What did Ambrose mean when he referred to two men? "Two men like yourself" certainly referred to gayness, men who knew Lambert and did what? Invite him to their place for photographs, coffee, and more? I told Ambrose that I knew that John was in jail.

"You know, what we're trying to do at this point is to persuade the city to reopen the investigation, reopen the case. The jury acquitted Haak and Wise so that means there is a killer out there. The so-called confessions the city obtained from Haak and Wise are questionable. And if they are questionable that means there is some type of police misconduct because it was the police…" Ambrose's voice trailed off when he was interrupted by his ringing phone.

I had not talked to Detective Tom Augustine at this point, although in the past I had had several experiences with the Philadelphia police that were not so good.

Everything's already been said, but since nobody was listening, we have to start again.

Andre Gide

In the mid-1970s, I experienced police harassment for walking or being in certain sections of Center City, such as when I was nabbed by a patrol wagon close to midnight for talking with a couple of guys on a stoop near a gay bar.

Inside the patrol wagon were ten gay men, all of them obviously picked up at random for the crime of walking in a well-known gay neighborhood. As the patrol wagon made its way through the streets, I had a small view of the street via a small screened air vent and heard the officers in the driver's seat say, "Let's get him." The "him" in this case was a particularly feminine-looking guy standing on a street corner. When the back of the wagon was filled with men, we all broke out in a chorus of "We Shall Overcome." At the police roundhouse, we were sent to individual jail cells, fed cheese sandwiches, and in the morning were brought before a judge and a gallery of spectators who laughed and jeered at us as the judge dismissed all charges.

This was a clear-cut case of police harassment, to be followed some months later when I was again ordered into the back of a police wagon late at night for no other reason than I had red hair. The police, it seems, were looking for a red-haired suspect, so I joined ten redheaded guys on the way to a police lineup under bright lights where hidden behind a one-way mirror the victim of a crime tried to ascertain which redhead was the guilty party. None of the assembled redheads in the lineup was selected. We were summarily dismissed and had to find out way home in the wee hours of the morning.

Ambrose hit a sympathetic note for me when he mentioned the checkered history of the Philadelphia Police. I then recalled how a cousin of mine, a university student, had been arrested for urinating in a dark alley away from public eyes after a night out at the bars. I also recalled the antics of the bike cops when they would harass anyone seen talking to the miscreants at 17th and Pine, or the poor sinner-saps like the author of this book who delighted in speaking with some of these people or even walking with them for a few blocks.

"Let me play devil's advocate here," I said to Ambrose, "and ask: do you think the police would actually force a confession and use brutality in such a highly publicized case? Wouldn't that be walking a dangerous tightrope?"

Ambrose was adamant. "Absolutely not, it's been known to happen many times before, and if you look at many cities throughout the country it happens surprisingly very often. And especially in high profile cases where they want to bring closure to this. One question I have for you, Thom. When you ... well, apparently after the murder took place you had an occasion to speak with John when you saw him..."

"I did."

"You noticed a change in his behavior?"

"It was very subtle. It was an attitudinal change, and I tapped into it. He didn't throw a teacup against the wall or punch out a window. It was very subtle. "

"But there was some subtle difference compared to his behavior before?"

"Yes."

"I think Skip Thomas mentioned to me that you and John were at one point walking outside your apartment right by the stairwell and John sort of froze or had some type of reaction to the stairwell?"

"You might read into it and say that it was a kind of delayed reaction of sorts. What we did was cross over to the stairwell side of Pine Street from my side and walked to the corner. I had given John a science fiction book that I wrote. He had it in his hands at that point and stopped at the corner to ask me about the book. I happened to be on my way to work and he was going to walk a few blocks down Pine with me and then go his way. For some reason he just stopped at the corner of 21st and Pine stairwell and we had a conversation."

"The stairwell isn't far back from that corner?" Ambrose asked.

"A few feet away," I answered, wondering where this was going.

"Did he make any reference to that stairwell or do any gesturing?"

"No, he did not. If he had I would remembered it. I had too much energy on the case to let something like that go by me. I had written about the case and was questioned about it."

"You were questioned about it by the Philadelphia Homicide Department?"

"Yes."

Ambrose asked me if I remembered which officers interviewed me, but I told him that I could not recall their names. I did clarify that there were two interviews, a short one and then a much longer one conducted by a different officer. The total interview time was about two hours. "After that I was driven home in a squad car. I got home late."

"Would the name Augustine sound familiar to you? Detective Augustine ... Thomas Augustine?"

"Augustine? That's a very Catholic sounding name ... I don't know," I said.

"He's far from being a saint," Ambrose said.

By this time Ambrose and I were on pretty friendly terms. "Saints are boring people anyway," I said.

"You know, I'll just throw out names to you to see if you recognize any of them. Detective Duzack?"

"Duzack sounds familiar," I said.

Of course, years later when I interviewed Augustine, he told me that the jogger case was originally Duzack's but that he became involved after Duzack asked him to transport John Hall to Graterford Prison. Ambrose then mentioned a Detective Boyle but that drew a blank. By now I was feeling so comfortable with Ambrose that I told him that the name "Boyle" sounded like something out of *Sherlock Holmes*. Ambrose threw out another name, Paul Musi.

"There should be a record of who talked to me at Homicide because the men I talked to took copious notes ... and yet when the attorney for Richie Wise called me and asked me testify he said that there was no record of my having been questioned on November 2, and he couldn't find any written record of my having gone down there to talk with anyone."

"Well, we do have a statement," Ambrose said. "We have a copy of the statement you gave to those detectives. Mr. Sam Malat, I guess, was referring to that. That's Mr. Wise's lawyer."

It made no sense to me why Ambrose was asking me who interviewed me at Homicide when he had a copy of the statement all along.

Ambrose asked if that was the only time that the detectives interviewed me. "They [Malat's people] called me two times asking me to come in for an interview. I was debating whether I should do it, so I asked for four or five days to mull it over."

"Why did you need time to mull it over?" Ambrose asked.

"Well, because Richard Wise was known in the media as a rabid homophobe. He had attacked a guy with a can of tuna fish and I had heard other things in the community about him. I also had a run in with him early one morning when he caught my eye—I happened to be looking at him—and he began threatening me. He was walking up Pine Street without a shirt on, strutting—the kind of walk that told you right away that this person has a huge chip on their shoulder and they are ready to snap. Agreeing to testify to help Wise was a problem for me because at the time I really felt that he was guilty ... and that he was acquitted because of a weird legal glitch, a circumstantial thing that sometimes happens. Or it could have been a dumb jury, I just don't know. I felt that justice had not been done and now this guy was trying to milk the city for money."

Ambrose corrected me and said that what he was asking me had to do with an interview the police wanted to do with me after the murder. "Why were you ambivalent about that?" What were your concerns at that point? This was back in '95–96."

"The police who arrested Wise and who were supposed to have forced a confession out of him and beat him up to me had the same stain as the police who accosted me that night on Pine on my way home from work when I was walking and talking this guy who happened to be a hustler. I was having a conversation with him, this hustler, just walking and talking, when a squad car pulled up out of nowhere, ordered us to the side of the car, and the officers drew their clubs like they were going to bash in skulls. We could have been mass murderers the way they were behaving. "

Ambrose wanted to know if, when I spoke to the guys who hung out at 17th and Pine, I ever mentioned to them that I knew John Lambert. I told Ambrose no. "Skip Thomas was the first one to bring John Lambert's name up," I said. "Up to that point I had never heard him in connection with Kimberly Ernest at all."

COFFEE WITH SKIP THOMAS

I had two interviews with Fred Ambrose, but almost immediately after the first interview Stephen Stouffer and Skip Thomas requested permission to visit with me in my Pine Street apartment. They also requested permission to tape the interview. I said they could do that if I could tape them taping me. They agreed to the arrangement.

The three of us gathered in my living room where Thomas did most of the talking. Stouffer, in fact, asked the first round of questions, but he did not want his part of the session taped. Thomas was the more laidback and taciturn of the two and seemed to be second in command as he often deferred to Stouffer. Stouffer had a hyper masculine component to his personality that bordered on the roughneck. In some ways, he impressed me as being a "grown up" version of the hustlers who hung out at 17th and Pine.

It was summertime when the two of them rang my bell. Stouffer was in shorts, just as he was the first time he paid me an unannounced visit. At that time, a friend driving me home from a long weekend in Long Island pulled up alongside my apartment building when I noticed a man in shorts and a tight t-shirt sitting on my steps. For a second I mistook him for one of the guys from 17th Street. Intuitively, I think I knew that he was waiting for me. As I got out of the car, he stood up and asked if I was Thom Nickels. I said I was.

He introduced himself as Stephen Stouffer, a private investigator for Fred Ambrose. I looked at him and tried to recall whether I had seen him in Ambrose's office. I did recall his face but his being in shorts changed his look somewhat. He asked if we could have a conversation in my apartment.

"Is there something wrong?" I asked.

I looked at my friend in the car and told him that the man was from Ambrose's office and wanted to talk with me in my apartment. I told him I did not know why he was here and that I would give him a call when we were finished.

In the apartment, Stouffer asked me a lot of questions about the noise I had heard in the wee hours of November 2, and about my "friendship" with John Lambert. He kept repeating the same questions, which annoyed me. He would return to these questions again and again as if trying to catch me in a lie. There were no tape recorders present during this visit. He asked if he and his PI partner, Skip Thomas, could come back and tape record a Q&A.

I had no idea what they wanted, but it seemed to me that they were digging for something. I also felt that the more I spoke with these guys, the deeper I was digging myself in some kind of a hole.

With both Stouffer and Thomas in my apartment, I went over the facts of the case from my perspective as they each took turns asking questions. By now I was pretty sick of answering the same questions over and over again. After Stouffer's relaxed first visit in which he seemed friendly, he was now more anxious and hard—mistrustful perhaps is a better word. As I would answer, I would get cock-eyed looks from him. He would make little grunts or reply in a sarcastic manner. Thomas, to his credit, behaved in a more civilized manner, but at times, even his politeness seemed to mimic Stouffer's emerging skepticism.

The session lasted two hours, and when they were gone, I thought that was the end of it. No more Stephen Stouffer and Skip Thomas. No more Fred Ambrose. There was not anything more to say anyway.

A little time passed and then I got a call from Thomas, who asked if he could come to my apartment without Stouffer. "Look, I realize you were under a little pressure from him. He's may not be the best interviewer, so I'd like to visit you alone if I could. You can record me as I record you if you want to."

I said yes, although I warned Thomas that I had said all I could say. "There are no new facts. We've been over this before." There had also been phone calls from Ambrose's team in the interim. Did I remember this? Are you sure about the time?

Are you sure you've told us everything? Like an orchestra climbing scales to reach a fever pitch, I felt the tone of the Ambrose team heating up. Sometimes Ambrose would call me with random questions then, before he hung up, he would say, "I might ask you to come to the office again."

Ambrose kept repeating that John Lambert had almost beaten his sister to death and that the city was trying to protect Lambert's father, a high-powered lawyer, in its refusal to reopen the case.

"I usually don't like to tape people right away. I like to talk to them a little bit and kind of break the ice somewhat," Skip Thomas told me when we were alone in my apartment. He was sitting on a single chair facing my Ikea sofa which at that point had springs that were slowly falling apart. I did not want him to sit on the sofa for fear the springs may snap and he would wind up on the floor. "Some people are a little gun shy," he added.

"You better not sit on the sofa, Skip."

Skip told me he wanted to go back to the first conversation we had. "There were a few questions I asked you. You had some recollection of seeing Billy that morning, or Billy and Johnny together. Is that correct?"

I never did see Billy or Johnny on the morning of the murder, and I thought that I had told Ambrose's team this, but as was their style, they liked to ask the same questions over and over even though the answers to those questions were given at an earlier date. "As I told you and Fred Ambrose before, I have no specific recollection of seeing them that day at all."

"Well, do you remember—let's go back a little bit further—do you remember the voices? Do you remember you told me you heard voices like yelling or screaming at people?"

Now I really felt that I was in caught in a stalled audio loop. Had my previous testimony gone unheeded? "Yes."

"Do you remember hearing a female voice or do you remember hearing a group of voices?"

"A group of voices that had a jolting sound, very sharp sounding, sharp enough to wake me up from a deep sleep. I don't usually wake up because of sounds on the street. For one thing, my bedroom door is made of cork and it blocks out a lot of sound. The bedroom is very quiet at night. I can't even hear traffic. It's almost like being in the country." Saying my bedroom door was made of cork made me think of Proust.

"But you heard sounds in the street that night?"

Was I speaking Russian? Should I suddenly change my testimony and say that I really heard nothing and that my previous claim that I had heard a chorus of voices was just a joke? "As I said, the sound caused me to sit up in bed and wonder, 'What was that?' It was that piercing…"

"Do you remember when you looked out your window that morning … do you remember seeing any female joggers on Pine?"

I did not tell Skip about the funny-looking woman who did the lesbian power walk, as some people called it, up and down Pine in the late afternoon. Stuart and I would often spot this woman power walking past the stairwell in a pair of large headphones. "I saw no female joggers on Pine early that morning," I said. "It was an extremely dark November morning. There was nobody on the street."

"It was a wet and dreary morning," Skip said. "But you didn't see a shadow or a figure outside?" Here he was again trying to get me to say that I saw Billy and John down around the stairwell.

"No, but in some ways I wish that I had. It would make this murder so much easier to solve. Of course, on some evenings before the murder I would see the Peeping Tom walking near the stairwell and Mr. Fineman's house, but I don't think he was trying to spy on Mr. Fineman. The Director of the Rosenbach Museum lives in the big house next to Mr. Fineman, but he lives there with his male partner. There'd be no reason for him to be hanging around the stairwell at 6 am."

Regarding the Peeping Tom, immediately after the killing, police were after any lead, so I told them about a tall thin red-haired man who would walk the Fitler Square area and peek into women's bedrooms. I'd seen him for a year or more, either late at night or in the wee hours of the morning. Usually he would lurk on the front steps of a row house pretending to be ringing a doorbell. Sometimes, when he thought no one was looking, he would cock his head at an angle, his eyes pressed into the window of a first-floor apartment.

Sometimes I would see him crouching down or leaning over as if working to see past some obstacle. With his tall bony body, he was a stereotypical, even comical, Peeping Tom. He must have made a list of "special" row houses because he would hit the same addresses over and over again.

A favorite house of his was across the street from me where a beautiful young woman had an apartment. Often I would wake up in the middle of the night, go to the kitchen to pour a glass of juice, and catch him glaring into her window.

He had persistence and nerve, but he was no killer. I am sure the police questioned him because after Ernest's murder I never saw him peeping on Pine Street again.

"Do you remember after the murder you said that John had come by to visit you? And that you stated that John seemed changed somehow?" Thomas asked.

"The last time John was here was after the murder, and I did notice a change in him," I said. "I somehow felt that he was a little less … nice."

"Nervous perhaps?" he prodded.

"He seemed to be somebody else."

"Do you recall seeing any scratches on John or any cuts on him at that time—on his face, on his arm, or on his hands? You may not have been looking for them..."

"I met John before the murder was committed. The last time he was here was long after the murder. He had no cuts or scratches."

"How about ... did you see Billy after that at some point? Did he look like he had been beaten up, scratched or cut?"

"Billy always gave me the impression that he was on the run and being chased by someone.... The last few times I saw him near 17th Street he had a panicked look in his eyes. I don't know whether that was caused by the drugs he was on.... I may be reading things into it now since you told me that he was with Lambert on the morning of the murder. I do know that when I saw him look at me the last time I saw panic in his eyes. Maybe this ties in to his statement that he had seen me up here by the window that morning..."

"Did John say anything about the murder, about Kimberly?" Skip asked. "You know, you said that he seemed strained, but did he actually get into any specifics about Kimberly or the murder especially considering that all the people around Pine Street were saying he murdered this girl?"

I had not heard that all the people around Pine Street were saying that he had murdered the jogger. This was news. By "people," of course, Skip Thomas meant the drug crowd and the hustlers at 17th and Pine. "As I said, I did walk John outside one day after I gave him a copy of my first book. We left the apartment building and crossed the street by the stairwell and then went to the corner when he stopped to ask me questions about the book. I do remember thinking at the time, 'Why is John choosing to have a conversation at this corner? For some reason I got the feeling that he wanted to be seen with me standing there."

"So you guys stopped at the corner of 21st and Pine for some reason? Well, going back to that morning, you said that it seemed like a strange kind of morning ... that things were out of the ordinary?"

"I did have a sense that something was different. It was just a feeling I had. Cold, dreary wet dark November morning, the kind of morning that makes you want to go back to bed."

"Now, you said that uniformed police officers came there to interview you initially. Did these officers ask you to describe what you saw or what you heard? I know you gave a statement, but do you remember anything specific that you may have forgotten at that point?"

"I wouldn't have held back anything," I said. "The first person I thought of was the red-haired Peeping Tom. I did mention him but in my gut I knew he was not the killer. He was just too ridiculous. Right after the murder one of the neighbors here complained that there was a black man sitting on the steps out here, but you probably have that information already.. I didn't feel that a black man sitting on the steps was anything."

"Did John say anything about the murder, or did you ask him anything about it?"

"Well, I'm sure we talked about it.... Somehow I remember him going over to my kitchen window when he was here and looking out at the street. I'm sure we had a conversation about the murder because everybody was talking about it. Everybody.... Two years after the murder people were still talking about it.... I got sick of talking about it."

At this point in our conversation, I heard my neighbor Allen come into the building. Apparently he had his friend with him because I heard them discussing something in the foyer. I assumed they came from the bar because their movements were clumsy, and you could hear one or both of them walking into furniture. How much of my conversation with Skip Allen could hear in his downstairs apartment was anybody's guess, but the walls at 2110 Pine were thin, so thin that I often heard my upstairs neighbors, a heterosexual couple, make love. The headboards of their bed would bang against the wall for the longest time, and her cries in the middle of the night sometimes kept me awake. My other upstairs neighbor, a twenty-something tall, blond educated guy named David, came to Philadelphia from the UK to work as an art restorer at the Philadelphia Museum of Art.

"Did anyone on the street or in the neighborhood ever tell you that John Lambert was the suspect or that John might have killed that girl?"

It struck me as odd that Ambrose's team kept referring to Kimberly Ernest as "that girl" as if the tragedy was a sitcom starring Marlo Thomas.

"No, never," I said. "I didn't really know that many people in the street."

Skip Thomas looked at me. "Never?" he said, as if I was holding something back. "The police never said anything about John Lambert?"

"The police only mentioned hustlers but never got specific. "

"That morning when you left for work ... what time did you say you left?" Thomas was beginning to sound tough, as if I was hiding something. Or maybe he was trying to ape Stephen Stouffer.

He began repeating questions. I tolerated the many repeats because I assumed that this was a technique that PIs learned in PI school, so I opted to play along without protest to see where it would all lead. But the questions were becoming boring and mundane.

"Around 6 a.m.," I said. "I was a little late that morning."

"So when you left here you walked on your side of the street?"

"Yes, I did although I felt an urge to cross the street and walk on the other side but I blocked that urge out and went straight down to 17th and Pine, took a left to Spruce and headed straight towards the Drake Apartments."

"At that point what did you see when you came out?"

"When I came out of the Drake?"

"No, your apartment."

"I saw nothing, just a damp quiet street with lots of fallen leaves on the sidewalks…"

"At that point did you think back to the noise that you heard earlier?"

I was now beginning to smell cooked fish from Allen's apartment. The smell was especially invasive and powerful. Was it the stink of Bluefish? I could not tell. It enveloped the building with a vengeance. Skip kept right on talking as if the smell was not there. It certainly was not the kind of cooking smell that would make anyone feel hungry.

"I thought of the noise I heard when I learned that there was a murder in the stairwell. When I left my apartment that morning I had not known about the murder although if I had crossed the street and looked into the stairwell I would have seen the body. After I learned of the murder and watched as they removed the body, I thought to myself, 'I heard this ruckus last night and I cannot believe that I'm the only one on the street who heard that noise at that time…"

"You're definitely not the only one who heard it," Skip Thomas said. "Unfortunately there are a couple of more people who just haven't come forward. So even if you came forward there's a whole lot more people that haven't."

I asked why anyone would remain silent about something like that.

"Well, certain people at that time heard the rumor that John killed the girl and they were afraid to come forward because they knew that John would be back on the street … so some of them are reluctant to come forward although two people came forward just recently. They were very helpful. Sometimes people don't know what to do. They panic. "

Yet police were asking neighbors if they had heard anything in the street months before John Lambert's name was ever associated with the case. Where were these neighbors then? It struck me as odd that Thomas was claiming, inferring, that these neighbors were keeping quiet because they feared that John Lambert would come back and attack them because they told the police they heard a noise. John Lambert's name at that time was only known to gay men, hustlers, and the drug subculture near 13th and Spruce and Locust.

"Two people did hear a female voice that morning," Thomas added. "And they did say similar things to what you said that they heard a couple of voices going back and forth. But they specifically remember a girl's voice. They remember a guy's voice but they definitely remember a female's voice."

Thomas then reconfirmed that there were no police records indicating any other problem near 21st and Pine on the morning of November 2.

"There were no cars broken into that morning. This was the only incident that happened that morning. We think that it might have been somewhere closer to 5:00 or a little bit after 5:00 am. But everybody's times are different. That's the problem. Your times are different from John's. John's times are different from Mike's."

By now the fish smell in Allen's apartment was toxic. Since Allen liked his fish burnt, there were light traces of smoke coming up to my apartment from his.

Allen's fish fry was the first smell that hit me when I moved to 2110 Pine in 1990. At that time it reminded me of the smell in a rooming house I lived in as a student near Baltimore's Park Avenue. This smell was a mix of mold, dirty socks, burnt food, and the stench of cigarettes. It is a smell that I have since come to associate with rooming houses, but especially the Baltimore house where across the hall from me was an older man in a room with a beveled glass door printed with the words "Fire Escape."

The old man played his AM radio day and night while the landlady, who lived on the first floor next to a young man about my age, encouraged me to introduce myself to this roomer whom she described as "a nice homosexual."

Her recommendation scared me to death. "Am I that noticeable?" I wondered.

The house at 2110 Pine was significantly better than that Baltimore rooming house. Allen, who had been a tenant since 1968, knocked on my door with a bottle of champagne when I moved to 2110 in 1990 and told me that an old man named Charlie used to live in my apartment. It is good to know the personal history of places.

6

JOHN LAMBERT AND BILLY LIBRATORE

Skip Thomas continued:

> I don't think too many people saw anything that morning or else we wouldn't be in this situation. So, it's kind of hard. You have to kind of weed out the people with too much imagination.
>
> Is there anything more that you can remember about that morning as far as seeing a body or even hearing anybody after you woke up or after you left your apartment? Any voices, any faces? I know you recall Billy and John. That's their normal time of hanging out, hanging around, but is there anything or anybody—was there a truck pulling over? Did you see a delivery truck? Did you see a car out of the ordinary? Did you see people out of the ordinary? The old man across the street, did you see him out that morning?

Was Thomas now targeting Mr. Fineman? In his rolodex of names, it seemed that everybody was a suspect, even though John Lambert was the Ambrose team's favorite candidate/suspect of choice.

"I was outside across the street from the stairwell before Mr. Fineman was out there," I said:

> Had I followed my instincts and crossed the street to the other side maybe I would have seen Kimberly in the bottom of the stairwell. But I did not. When I returned from work, Mr. Fineman was there with his dog, so I was the second

person on the scene. Mr. Fineman told me that there was somebody injured in the stairwell and he was waiting for the police. He did not say the person was dead. Maybe he didn't know that. I assumed the person in the stairwell was a homeless man who had somehow fallen in there. Immediately after Mr. Fineman told me this several patrol cars pulled up. For weeks following the murder Mr. Fineman could be found out on the sidewalk talking to people about the murder. He'd become a tour guide of sorts…

"Did John mention a friendship or a relationship with Kimberly?"

That idea seemed foreign to me because John was a street hustler, albeit a soft-spoken one with obvious good breeding, and Kimberly worked in a law firm, was heterosexual, and did not hang out in the street. What I failed to consider then was how the world of drugs at that time might have brought them together if only in a superficial way in the gay bars at 13th and Locust.

"John never said he knew her," I said. "I'm sure that when I talked about the murder with him I mentioned that I used to see her jog."

"When you saw her jog, did she jog across the street by the stairwell?" Thomas asked.

"I once saw her jog on the stairwell side of the street coming back from the river, but usually it was on my side of the street. I'm sure she jogged both ways just as all joggers do."

I asked Thomas what Kimberly was wearing when she was murdered. "She wore a black top, a jogging bra and jogging pants and sneakers—and a walkman. Did you ever notice her with the walkman?"

"Yes, the walkman over her shock of hair. She had a lot of hair."

"Listen," Thomas said, glancing at his beeper and mentioning that Stouffer was contacting him, "Has anyone else contacted you since we've been talking, the police or anybody, attorneys, anybody besides the coroner? And official contacts from attorneys, or police or city officers?"

"Nothing like that," I said, "although I did have a dream that my apartment had been ransacked."

"Well, let's hope that doesn't ever happen," Thomas said. "You'll have real problems if that happens…. Did you know John by a street name … John McHugh?"

"I didn't know John McHugh, just John Lambert."

"And John was always with Billy?"

"Of course not…. John was often by himself."

"By himself?" Thomas seemed to think this was hard to believe.

"I saw him with Billy one time when he got in a car on Pine Street with another man whom I had heard was a drug pusher. Billy was sitting on somebody's stoop watching them."

"Well, you said that you sometimes saw them together in the morning?"

"Not together, but separately," I stated.

"But you'd see them both at some point in the mornings?"

"Very often … this time Billy was sitting on the steps on Pine watching John go into a car occupied by this other guy. I guess John was going in the car to get high. John hid being high very well. I never saw him do anything wacky in public. He always seemed to be in control. He certainly wasn't anything like Billy."

"Billy was loose cannon?"

"John was low key, cerebral, but he could be very, very pushy."

The smoke from Allen's burnt fish had by now set off the fire alarm. Thomas stood up as if it was a real emergency but I told him to take a seat. "My neighbor always burns his fish and the neighbors pay little attention to it," I said.

I heard Allen's door open, and then the outer doors to the street, and knew that he and his friend were letting in fresh air to try and stop the alarm. Later I learned that Allen and his friend Reilly had fallen asleep after putting on the fish and were scrambling about doing damage control.

Thomas asked if he could use my phone to call Stouffer.

I left the apartment briefly while he did that to check on Allen's situation. Allen and Reilly were standing by the mailboxes in the foyer. Allen was holding the still-smoking frying pan filled with two chunks of what looked like black embers. A very drunk Reilly could barely stand up. Allen set the frying pan on the top step outside and apologized for the commotion.

Thomas had completed his call by the time I got back upstairs. I knew the call was a report on what Thomas and I had been talking about. "I want to pursue the pushy element. You said John could be very pushy," Thomas said.

"He could be. He was the kind of person who could talk himself into inviting himself over to your place for coffee and then once at your place give off vibes that he didn't want to be there. He was strong willed."

"You know, the last time we talked I asked if you thought John was capable of murder. I guess maybe that's the way we'll end our conversation today with that same question."

"On the surface, serial killers can have a really sweet 'tea and sympathy' personality. This makes it hard to see beneath the surface. Men like Richie Wise might appear more as killer types—you know, the wild man acting out in the street and quick to lose his temper, whereas John's personality was always under wraps, wrapped in velvet gloves...."

I said that both personality types could easily be murderers.

The Ambrose team was floating the story that Kimberly met John on the morning of the murder at 17th and Pine Streets where they had some kind of altercation. An argument ensued and John followed her up to the stairwell.

"Have you ever seen John argue with anybody?" Thomas asked.

I told him that when I saw John enter the car while Billy sat on a nearby stoop I got the feeling that I should not invite John into my apartment anymore. "He was a loner. He stayed by himself. The people around him, the 17th Street crowd, would always talk about police harassment but John never talked about trouble with the cops."

"You mentioned that John almost always seemed like he had an ace in the hole, and obviously that ace in the hole is his father."

"Right," I replied. "He could go to his father for protection. And so he must have felt very secure..."

"Did John ever mention that he had any type of important information that no one else had, some information about something mob related or drug related or politically related, something that he knew that nobody else knew, a secret he had?"

Something was happening to me. I falling under the spell of Skip Thomas' repeat questions. The chronic repetitions were making me doubt the truthfulness of my own answers, second guessing what I saw and felt. The net effect of all this was that I was beginning to look at John Lambert in a totally different way.

"I wouldn't be surprised if John Lambert had a secret," I said. "I got a sense of layers with him, layers of secrets, that sort of thing. I also got the feeling that he was not telling the whole story. I should also say that, really, I don't think I ever really completely trusted him from the very beginning."

"There's definitely something hidden beneath all of his layers," Thomas said. "I don't have any more questions. That's it for me."

"Is the evidence you have against John pretty solid now?' I asked.

"Pretty solid ... there is very solid evidence against John."

"Does John know that all of this is happening and that very soon he's going to be placed in the center of events?"

"That is correct."

With that, Skip Thomas left the apartment.

By now the shrine in front of the stairwell had been dismantled, yet I would occasionally take a look at it and recall the morning of November 2. Fred Ambrose still called me periodically, insisting that he had more questions and asking me to come to his office. My editors at *Au Courant* had no further interest in the case.

They felt that we had covered everything there was to cover and essentially they were correct. My time with Ambrose was no longer tied to official reporting, although my sense was that perhaps my continued talks with him might lead to something down the road.

Yet I was beginning to feel a sense of dread about these interviews. The repeat questions had somewhat of a diabolical tone. How many times can you say the same thing over and over again? It became obvious to me that the Ambrose team was after something else. It was becoming clear that they thought I was more involved than I was, yet I remained firm in my decision to play along and see where things went.

At no point did Ambrose offer me even a cup of coffee during our visits. When our sessions ended, that was that. I left the office and took the next bus into Center City. Stephen Stouffer once drove me home although my sense of things at that time was that the PI was acting in a slightly provocative way, as if he wanted me to act in an untoward manner. This is how I read his body language in any event. I suspected that he wanted me to come onto him so he would have some kind of advantage, but what kind of advantage? The whole ordeal was becoming stranger and stranger.

At his Bala Cynwyd office, Ambrose picked up where he left off the last time I was there. He wasted little time. His behavior and questions were by now all very mechanical. He went back to John Lambert and how many times I had seen Lambert and Billy Libratore at 21st and Pine Streets.

"21st and Pine is outside the loop," told him. "So it wouldn't be too often that I saw anybody at 21st who hung out at 17th and Pine. Sometimes I'd see John Lambert around Town Pizza at 19th and Pine. That's about as far up as he would go."

Skip Thomas entered the room, appearing out of nowhere it seemed.

"So you don't remember ever seeing John at 21st and Pine before or after the murder?" Ambrose repeated for the 100th time.

"No, John only came to 21st and Pine where I lived when I invited him, and that was only two or three times and some months apart at that..."

"John would come to your apartment. Visit you," Ambrose said.

"Sometimes I'd see him on my way home from my morning job. He'd come back with me for coffee. One time I gave him a copy of my science fiction book."

Ambrose lit a cigar. "Do you know anything about John's background, his family or anything? Did you ever discuss any of these things with him?"

"I was told he had a brother, I think a twin. John was not part of the regular circle at 17th and Pine. He seemed to have an off-site existence. He had a life of his own which set him apart from the guys down there."

"What do you mean by that?"

"He wasn't your average dim-witted hustler. He had a detached air. He had an interest in books and ideas. For a person who hung out a lot in the street, these things about him really stuck out."

Ambrose wanted to know if John ever mentioned anything about his father or mother. "I believe his mother is a doctor," Ambrose said.

"He didn't offer any information. He was pretty vague when it came to his family but he was always asking me a lot of questions. He talked about his so-called brother and he talked about living with somebody, and I talked to him about struggling to get money. Once or twice he talked about his father who helped him out financially. There were references to his father and his father sending him money when he was between jobs, things like that."

"Other than John visiting with you at your place did you ever have an opportunity to visit with him at his apartment?"

"No, we were not tied together that way. I'd usually meet John accidentally when I passed through that area, and I did that a lot, at least four times a day. John would be standing on the corner. He'd be by himself and he'd call my name and then invite himself to walk with me. It was no big deal to invite him in for coffee. But he wasn't anybody I sought out. I didn't even have his phone number. I wouldn't have called him anyway because I wasn't all that interested. It was all just a chancy thing."

"How about this Billy Libratore? He's known as Billy on the street. I think you know who I am referring to."

"I've seen him on the street," I told Ambrose.

"What did you first notice about him?"

I described how Libratore acted in the street without mentioning that I really felt bad for him and that despite his external craziness I felt there was a good person *underneath*. "A seemingly pathetic, out of control guy," I told Ambrose. "He was always racing around in the street approaching cars and running up to strangers without trying to discern whether somebody was interested in him.... A loose cannon posing as the village idiot, but maybe he wasn't an idiot."

"Ever see Billy in the company of John?"

"I told Skip Thomas that the last time I saw John, Billy was near him on a stoop. John was walking towards a parked car. John's brother was in the driver's seat. I said hello to John then did a double take when I saw someone who looked just like John in the car. Billy saw my reaction and said, 'Yeah, his twin sells drugs," and I said, 'Oh, that's nice...'"

"So you did see John's brother, or at least get a glimpse of him?"

"It was just a side profile. What I saw was a tall, skinny guy with long hair who looked just like John."

"Did you know what his brother's name was?" I told Ambrose no, after which he asked if anybody besides his team had ever brought up John's name with me in connection with the case. To that I also replied no.

"Did you ever speak to Leonard Wise, that's Richie Wise's brother," Ambrose asked. "Did he ever speak to you?"

But Leonard Wise was not Richie Wise's brother, but his father. How could Ambrose not know this? How could he have gotten this wrong?

"Is there anything else you remember about John? I'm just trying to pick your brain about your encounters with him…. Is there anything that seems small and insignificant to you, but might mean something to us?"

"I did get the impression that John came from a very good family and that there was a part of him that saw his time on the streets as slumming it. He also appeared to be a nice guy … he smiled easily, always said hello and good-bye with a handshake, was calm and tranquil. His feathers never seemed to ruffle."

"Did you ever see him use drugs?"

"I assumed he did some kind of drug, all those guys did but in the beginning I never suspected heroin."

"Getting back to Billy…" But why was Ambrose "getting back to Billy?" The fact that Ambrose was paying so much attention to Billy seemed to deflate his credibility. Billy was a circus clown, a buffoon. "Other than what you've already said," Ambrose continued, "do you recall any other encounters with him or any other information about Billy?"

I felt that Ambrose really wanted to know if I had had any sexual connection to Billy but he was afraid to ask that question directly. The fact that he was pestering me with repeat questions about Billy suggested he really wanted a sexual tidbit or two. He was hoping that I would get the hint and give in. He obviously did not want to go on record with direct questions in this regard.

"Billy would run up to me in the street and ask if I would take him home. He wanted me to buy him but I was not interested. He couldn't take no for an answer and he would not give up."

Ambrose went back to John. "Did you ever come to a point where you had to ask John to leave your apartment?"

"No, John was in my place for relatively short amounts of time. I do remember noticing a subtle change in his behavior the last time he was with me, and I didn't like it. It was the last time he was ever in my place."

"At that point had you become fearful of him in any way?"

"It wasn't fear, it was an attitude I didn't like, a pushiness I'd never seen before. I thought it might be indicative of something happening in his life."

Skip Thomas jumped in. "You said that right after the murder you saw Billy, and that Billy was even worse, and you said that John was even worse than you had ever seen him." This was an obvious reference to the fact that both John and Billy looked worse because they had just murdered Kimberly Ernest and were suffering the after effects of that deed. "You also said that Billy looked scared and afraid during one of your conversations with him. Did you attribute that to anything? You did say that John and Billy were definitely different afterwards, that John looked like he was falling apart..."

"John did look disheveled but I have to be careful here because that could have been from the drugs. He might have taken too much and was on a bender as they say."

"What about Billy?" Thomas asked.

What about Billy? I was beginning to hear this question as a song title: What About Billy; What About Billy in the Morning; Where Did Billy Go After the Rain Stopped?

I repeated what I had said about Billy before. There was nothing new to add. "Billy's behavior was not unique. I've seen behavior like this at 17th and Pine. I mean kids are out there and maybe they fall asleep on somebody's stoop, or they do crazy things like run into traffic trying to flag cars down.... It is true that the last few times I saw Billy he seemed more frantic than usual. But again, you attribute this to too many drugs. He seemed to be on a non-stop drug roll. The last time I saw him was a long time after Kimberly was killed, maybe two years ago..."

"It's 1997 now," Ambrose said. "Kimberly died in '95."

"So you didn't see John or Billy until a long time after the murder then?" Thomas asked.

"I knew them both before the murder, of course."

"You said that one of the times you saw John was right after the murder when he actually walked over to the kitchen window in your apartment as everyone else did who was in your place at that time because, well, you know, you were the center of attention," Skip Thomas said.

"Look, I'm not putting you on the spot. I'm just trying to go back and create a time line here. That's what we're doing. It's not that we're picking on you. You're an intelligent man and you can be very helpful to us. It's not to obsess on John. It's just to get this thing in order. But you do remember that John went up to your kitchen window shortly after the murder. So maybe you saw John immediately after the murder and then after that you didn't see him for a while and then you saw him maybe six months to a year later?"

"When you talk about John going up to my window, Skip, that in no way implies a Pontius Pilate washing of the hands, like going back to the scene of the crime and examining your conscience ... because everybody I knew, family and friends who came to visit me, went to my kitchen window and pondered the stairwell across the street. It was what people did in my apartment."

"You could have charged admission," Thomas quipped.

"So, because everybody I knew gazed out my window and talked about the stairwell, the fact that John did it didn't arouse my suspicions at all."

"Sir," Ambrose broke in, "What do you remember about the morning of November 2nd?"

The use of the word "sir" by Ambrose was interesting. It implied formality, detachment, even looking at me through a different sort of lens. "Do you remember hearing or seeing or whatever? What do you remember about it? I know you told Skip and Steve about this and probably many others many times, but if you can tell me I would appreciate it."

Ambrose would not give up trying to catch me in a lie.

"Well, in the wee hours before dawn I was jolted awake by a horrific scream, a number of screams that were sharp and piercing. They made me sit up in bed..."

"When you say sharp and piercing do you mean a voice?"

"Human voices.... It was definitely more than one voice, maybe two or three. They were very sharp and woke me out of a sound sleep. When I didn't hear any follow up screams, breaking glass or police sirens, such as you'd hear if there had been a car accident or a fire, I went back to sleep. After those screams there was just dead silence. I thought the whole thing was probably nothing."

Ambrose asked me if I was able to make out any of the words that were being spoken.

"This was a frantic scream, no words, very intense and jolting and then there was nothing."

"If you were to take a stab at trying to guess how many voices you might have heard, would you say it was two voices or more than two voices?" Ambrose asked.

"Two or more voices," I said.

"Was it a combination of male and female voices?"

"It could have been anything, a combination," I offered.

"What was your sense at the time if you could remember that? What feeling did you get? Do you get an impression when you hear something?"

I told Ambrose that I got a sense of something really extreme, something out of the ordinary. "That's what flashed through my mind ... something out of control ... extreme rowdiness."

While answering Ambrose's questions, I regretted not leaving the bedroom after hearing the screams and checking the street to see what was going on. All I had to do, after all, was walk to the kitchen window and peer out into the street while being careful not to turn the lights in the apartment on.

Had I done that, what would I have seen? Would I have spotted John Lambert in his hippie pony tail throwing Kimberly Ernest into the stairwell, as Billy Libartore walked frantically in circles, or would I have seen Richie Wise and Herbert Haak dragging Kimberly into the stairwell? Perhaps by the time I had gotten to the window the murderers would have fled and I would not have seen anything. My second-story window was not high enough to see into the bottom of the stairwell so perhaps the most that I would have seen, had I gotten out of bed and rushed to the window, would have been a couple of figures moving up and down the stairwell, then escaping into the night. I might have gotten a glimpse of the murderer(s). I would certainly have recognized Richie Wise with his platinum blond hair, and John Lambert's distinctive pony tail would have been an easy indicator. Haak, of course, was more of a generic blob with his fire plug shaped body.

And what if the murderers had seen me at the window?

Or what if I had actually left the apartment building and gone outside and stood on my stoop, or gone over to the stairwell and, assuming the murderer(s) were still there, announced that they had better stop or I would call the police? Would they then run across the street and attack me as they had attacked Kimberly Ernest? Vicious killers of this caliber were liable to do anything, so lumping several bodies into the stairwell is not really too farfetched of an idea considering the gruesomeness of this case.

Would a phone call to the police had I seen something that morning saved Kimberly Ernest? Or did the screams come at the exact moment that Kimberly Ernest died? And why did I hear a chorus of screams; why would the murderer(s) be screaming?

I did not like not knowing the answers to these questions.

Ambrose asked me if I recalled anything else on the morning of November 2 after I woke up.

"That morning I went into the kitchen and turned on the light above the sink," I told Ambrose. "As I mentioned to Skip, I probably took a quick glimpse out the window either before or after I turned the light on. Then I put the coffee on. It was a very dark, dreary morning, very damp. I drank my coffee in the living room on the sofa by the telephone where I had a view of the big bay window that also faces the stairwell. It was a very quiet morning."

"What time was that, roughly?" Ambrose asked.

"I'd say anywhere from 6 to 6:30 a.m."

Skip Thomas asked my permission to record this part of the interview but the irony is that Ambrose was already recording everything although I was not aware of that.

"I'm going to have an opportunity to ask questions, right Fred?" I asked. This was the first time that I used Ambrose's first name.

The fact is, I cannot say the name "Fred" without thinking of Fred Flintstone or the actor Fred McMurray. In many ways, people over time become the names they are given at birth, and Fred Ambrose certainly looked like some sort of "Fred" from the cavalcade of "Freds" whirling about in my mind: cartoon Freds, pancake-shaped face Freds, men who were almost never handsome but had some odd facial characteristic that made you remember them. Ambrose was a short man who wore giant German-style aviator glasses which also made me think of a praying mantis. He was definitely a "Fred."

"You may ask a question that may help us," Thomas said.

Then Thomas and Ambrose got into a discussion about tape recorders. "What size tape do you want to use?" Ambrose asked Thomas. "I got a big tape machine or do you want to use a small cassette? Let me see if I have a small."

"While he's doing that, ask me some questions," Thomas said. "What do you want to know?"

The unseen tape recorder was still recording all of us, but where was it?

"I want to know about the connection between John and Kimberly," I said. "Why would Kimberly have gotten involved with a common street hustler?"

Ambrose, who was now using the small cassette, said, "These are my theories: Kimberly, from what we have been able to find out, and for lack of a better word, had a checkered sort of background. She, like all young people, I guess, get involved in the drug scene or the louder side of life. For instance, we understand that just before her death she was getting herself straightened out trying to get back in shape physically, emotionally, and get her career going. She wanted to be a paralegal, had recently gotten a job as a paralegal, and so I think that it was while she was in her wild phase that she may have encountered either John and/or people like him, similar to the ones you've been describing to me at 17th and Pine Streets."

"Look," Ambrose continued, "It's hard to investigate a person's life who is deceased, especially going back two—almost three—years now, but from what we've been able to piece together that's what we've been able to find out. She went through that phase and drinking—a lot of clubbing, nightclubs. She got into the scene where these young people hang out, the bars downtown, some of the shadier bars and so on. I think that's how she met people like John."

"When you say shadier bars, what do you mean?"

"Oh bars down there like…" Ambrose turned to Thomas and asked him the names of some of the shadier bars down there "in that area we were going through."

Thomas mentioned Westbury and Dirty Frank's but especially the latter which he called "a big place for her."

"Dirty Frank's isn't really shady," I said. "It's boring. And they serve bad wine. It's a pseudo bohemian hangout with lots of drugs, I hear. The Westbury is not shady at all. It was known for its good food."

I then asked Ambrose why someone like Billy was being seen as Lambert's accomplice. "Are you actually accusing him of having a hand in the murder or being just a lookout?"

"I'm only accusing John of doing all of this," Ambrose said. "Right now we're trying to gather evidence that's all in Municipal Court. Let me put a caveat on that, however. I can't answer any more questions on that particular issue. A lot of our sources are confidential and I really can't give you that information."

"About John, you mean?"

"This case is done and when it's opened—and I really believe the City will reopen this case and they will charge John Lambert with this murder. At that point I'll be glad to give everybody all the information that we'd be able to give. Right now I can't say when this will be."

Skip Thomas got up from his chair and walked around the room.

"I just wanted to go back on certain things that are still sticking out in my mind, and it's the time frame of the morning. Can you just go over your time line in the morning again, only because we're comparing different people who we are interviewing who have slightly different time lines? Can you just go back and start from when you heard the sound to maybe when you fell back asleep. Just start from there and go forward…"

"I heard the sound before the time on the original police report that stated when she died. The attack is listed as having occurred somewhere at 5:40 a.m. at 18th and Pine. I heard the sound in the wee hours of the morning, before dawn. It could have been 3, 4:30 or 5:00 a.m., I don't know. I did not look at my clock."

"So anytime before 7:00 a.m. It was raining and drizzling out then," Thomas said.

"It was well before 7:00 a.m. because I went back to sleep. My alarm hadn't gone off yet. It went off at a quarter to 6, so it was some time before 5:30 when I heard the sound. I never understood why the police never questioned me about the noises I heard. I told two detectives about the screams and it seemed to go right past them. They seemed to think it wasn't significant. They never re-questioned me about it. Certainly if I were a detective I would have pursued that. But the noise, the screams—it was a jolting thing that caused me sit upright in bed out of a sound sleep. What kind of noise does this?"

Ambrose swiveled around in his big leather armchair.

"Let me ask you this, Thom: if there was any altercation between two or more people anywhere between that Van Pelt Street area and going across Pine to where the stairwell is, would you have heard it, assuming they were arguing with each other—words being spoken in a higher than normal tone—would you have heard that from your apartment?"

"In the middle of the night Pine Streets acts as a kind of canyon," I said. "Sound reverberates. I can sit in my living room and hear the conversations of people walking outside the apartment. It's not an eavesdropping thing at all; the conversations just pour into your lap."

"But if you were asleep in your bedroom with the door closed that would be a different situation, would it not?"

"Yes, I would not have been able to hear any conversations at all. It's a fairly soundproof door. It cuts out a lot of noise. It's a cork door."

I was going to mention to Ambrose that my cork-lined door cut out noise as effectively as Marcel Proust's cork-lined bedroom and writing room cut out noise in his house at Boulevard Haussmann, Paris. I held my tongue, however.

"When you knew John back then," Ambrose asked, "Did he normally have a ponytail?"

"Once in a while he would have it hanging, but rarely. Usually it was in a ponytail."

Ambrose wanted to know if I had ever seen John in jogging outfits or jogging type pants or sweatshirt type things and hooded shirts. I told him that John usually wore loose-fitting clothing and that his clothing stood out.

"When I think of John I think of someone in sweats—gray or green in color, everything seemed to drape on him although he was not overweight at all but, as you know, tall and slender." When I said the words "drape on him" I thought of the Moo Moo's that Mama Cass wore, the flowing tents that seemed to lend some grace to her obesity.

"How about jewelry?" Ambrose asked. "Did you ever notice him wearing some type of jewelry, rings or bracelets or pendants or watches?"

John was certainly no Guido-type runner for the Mafia, decked out in gold chains and heavy doses of cologne. The question stunned me and I wondered why Ambrose asked it. What was he getting at? "I never saw him in jewelry," I said.

"Ask me a question now," Ambrose said.

"Do you think that the police knew that John Lambert was the real killer when they had Wise and Haak in custody? At what point did this supposed cover-up begin?"

Ambrose took a very serious tone. "What makes you think we're focusing on a cover-up? Did somebody discuss it with you or are you just speculating, or..."

"I'm asking because there's an implication that the law firm that John Lambert's father is part of has something to do with protecting John Lambert. At what point did this protection or cover up begin, do you know?"

"There was some speculation that John's father, the powerful lawyer whose law firm has connections to the City, is doing everything in his power to prevent the prosecution of his son."

"When did the police first decide that they wanted to solve this case real fast?" Ambrose asked me. The question was rhetorical. "That occurred anywhere between mid-November of '95 until the end of November. I think that from November 2 until the middle of the month the investigation was going like a normal homicide investigation would go. And then things started to happen and in my opinion derailed from the normal course to some other course. My opinion is that Haak and Wise were framed," Ambrose continued. "The confessions were either a combination of coercion and fabrication, and fabrication is quite different from coercion."

We very quickly went from that to discussing the original report of death. I mentioned that it was around 5:40 a.m. Ambrose countered with, "The original time of death according to what the police found out ... there was a truck driver in that area around 6:10 a.m. who saw Kimberly jogging at around 21st and Pine at that point..."

If that was true, then the screams I heard on the morning of November 2 were unrelated to Kimberly's murder. But how was this possible? Later, when I spoke with Kimberly's mother, Dorothe Ernest of Illinois, I was informed that Kimberly began her jog every day at 5:30 a.m. Would it have taken Kimberly forty minutes to jog from her apartment at 1105 Spruce Street to 21st and Pine?

Or perhaps she got a late start on her jog that morning. Who was this truck driver anyway? I had read references to a truck driver who claimed he saw Kimberly jogging at that time in various newspaper accounts, but the claim seemed antidotal and unreal.

Ambrose continued. "So Kimberly was at 21st and Pine or approaching the area at about 6:10. So her attack occurred anywhere between 6:10 and when her body was found which was 7:40. So the attack took place during that time frame. I can't pinpoint it any more specifically."

"But these times would have been well after I heard the shouts," I said.

"Well, I think there may have been things leading up to the actual attack," Ambrose rejoined.

"I think Skip or Steve told you that Billy said he saw John at 17th and Pine and saw John encounter Kimberly in that area—this happened at around quarter to six or ten of six or so. And it's our speculation that that John continued this encounter with her from that area down to 21st Street, and then another altercation took place and that led to what happened to her."

"That's why I was asking you the other day about the direction she was running in," Thomas blurted out.

"Where did the truck driver see her, which side of the street did the truck driver see her?" I asked.

"Offhand, I think he said he was driving up Pine Street and Pine Street runs east ... and there is the stairwell on the north side. And I think he was driving down there and saw her coming down the north side of Pine. He saw her going across that corner on 21st Street running along Pine on the north side, I think."

"So Kimberly jogged past the stairwell towards the river in the westward direction?" I reiterated that I had seen her jogging only a few times in the afternoon, not in the early morning. I also said that the first time I walked past her while she was jogging it was on my side of Pine Street when she was headed west towards the river. There were one or two times that I would spot her jogging back from the river on the north side of the street past the stairwell.

"When you saw her what was she normally wearing, what kind of clothing?" Ambrose asked.

"The first time I saw her, not much clothing at all. Maybe a black tank top, very tight and form fitting. I remember thinking, 'Wow, how skimpy!'"

"What kind of pants?"

"I don't recall the pants. I just remember the tank top being very low cut. She stood out because her thick red hair was flying all around."

Ambrose asked if when I saw her if her hair was in "one of those things you put on a ponytail." "What do you call that?" he wanted to know.

"It was not a French bun. Her hair when I saw her was always down but held back somehow so it didn't get in her face. Her hair was massive, beautiful. Amazon curls."

Thomas asked me how tall I thought she was. "She seemed tall for a woman, but I don't know. Maybe the large headphones she wore made her look taller." (Dorothe Ernest would tell me later that her daughter was 5 feet 8 inches.)

"Okay, it's your turn to ask questions," Ambrose said.

"So you think that John waited for her return jog from the river back to her apartment, or do you think that he followed her down to 21st and Pine where he waited for her? I was checking that area out earlier and noted that there are few places to hide."

Ambrose agreed that the stairwell where the body was found was really the only hiding place on the block. I suggested that perhaps John might have found an open apartment house door and hid in there, and that once he spotted her he ran out into the street. The outer doors to several of the apartment houses on the block were sometimes left open, as was the case at 2110 Pine when a tenant for whatever reason unlocked the automatic lock mechanism.

"Again, we're speculating since we can't really say. When I examined the area I found that the stairwell is really the only good hiding place. Then there's Van Pelt Street on your side of the street ... that's a good location, so that's a possibility."

"John's father is part of a law firm that is very, very powerful and it has great influence in City Hall, right?"

"He's a partner in the firm Duane, Morris & Heckscher which has been in the area for many, many years, generations even, and there are several branch offices..."

"How would John's father wield so much power as to thwart an investigation?"

"I didn't say that he's thwarted the investigation," Ambrose said. "We are concerned about the father because he is a managing partner in the firm and it's a very influential law firm. It is closely connected with the City and he has done a lot of work for the City. He still does a lot of work for the City. So there is a lot of political power there."

"So there are no formal accusations at this time?"

"I haven't accused anybody of anything yet except John Lambert," Ambrose said:

I've accused John Lambert of killing Kimberly Ernest. I'm interested in showing what really happened here. I mean this girl is dead. She was brutally killed and the person who did that should be brought to justice and the people that helped to delay justice being done should also be brought to task. I was going to use the word "cover up" and I think those people should be brought to justice.

So that's my goal right now. If I don't get a cent out of this case for my client, if I don't earn a cent out of this case for a fee, as long as I'm able to show who is really guilty of this murder and what happened, I'll be as happy as a lark. You know, I have a daughter and it could easily have happened to her as to Kimberly, and if it did I would certainly hope somebody would pry open the truth and not let it sit the way it's been sitting here for almost three years.

Ambrose did not sound like someone who would have a daughter, so I was surprised by that statement, just as I was about his altruistic claim that he did not

Center City, Philadelphia, at night, *c*. 1995. (*Courtesy of the author*)

21st and Pine Street, *c*. 1912. The stairwell where Kimberly Ernest's body was found on November 2, 1995, is partially hidden (on the right) behind a barrier. (*Courtesy of the author*)

Tom Augustine, the Philadelphia detective who interrogated Herbert Haak. Augustine was charged with crimes that he did not commit. (*Courtesy of Tom Augustine*)

Kimberly Ernest as a college student. (*Courtesy of Dorothe Ernest*)

Kimberly Ernest about the time she was enrolled in paralegal school in Philadelphia. (*Courtesy of Dorothe Ernest*)

Dorothe Ernest in 1995.
(*Courtesy of Dorothe Ernest*)

Inmate Number: EG5803

Name	Name Type	Image
HERBERT HAAK	Commit Name	
HERBERT CARL HAAK	Also Known As	
HERBERT-CARL PAUL HAAK III	True Name	
ROBERT HAAK	Also Known As	

12/5/2017 9:06:55 AM

Age: 47

Date of Birth: 10/06/1970

Race: WHITE

Height (in): 5' 09"

Gender: MALE

Citizenship: USA

Complexion: FAIR

Current Location: DALLAS

Permanent Location: DALLAS

Committing County: PHILADELPHIA

Last Updated Time: 8/23/2018 4:00:17 AM

Inmate details, Herbert Haak. (*Courtesy of Tom Augustine*)

Richard Bryan Wise

May 19, 1976 - September 6, 2016

Richard Bryan Wise, 40 of Mays Landing, passed from life to life eternal on September 6, 2016. Richard was born and raised in Philadelphia, Pa. He was employed by Lyons Security and worked at the Atlantic City Race Course. Richard was a wonderful man with a great heart. He loved spending time with family and friends. His Goddaughter Abbey was his little princess.

He is predeceased by the loves of his life, daughter, Alyssa and her Mom, Kelly Juhas; his father Leonard; and his brother, Christopher.

He is survived by his mother, Theresa (Josh) of Sweetwater; his brother, Eric (Antonia) and their daughters, Abigail and Kaelen, all of Mays Landing; Grandmother Eva E. Harbison of Sweetwater; and his nephew, Ian. He also leaves behind many Aunts, Uncles, cousins and friends who loved him very much.

A Celebration of Richard's life will be held on Thursday, September 15, 2016 at Wimberg Funeral Home, 400 Liverpool Avenue, Egg Harbor City, NJ. Visitation will be from 11:00 am until noon with a service immediately following. Internment at Egg Harbor City Cemetery. In lieu of flowers, A Go Fund Me Page has been set up to help the family with funeral expenses.

Richard Wise obituary, 2016. (*Courtesy of Tom Augustine*)

Phyllis Hall, mother of Herbert Haak, on the porch of her home. (*Courtesy of Tom Augustine*)

John Hall, stepfather of Herbert Haak and notorious jailhouse snitch. (*Courtesy of Tom Augustine*)

ANM: tnl
DJ 144-62-2083

Washington, D.C. 20530

November 01, 1999

Mr. Thomas J. Augustine
12611 Dunksferry Road
Philadelphia, Pennsylvania 19154

Dear Mr. Augustine:

The Civil Rights Division of the Department of Justice recently completed its review of an investigation as reported by the Federal Bureau of Investigation. This matter concerned allegations that you were involved in a criminal violation of civil rights statutes regarding the deprivation of the civil rights of Herbert Haak.

After a careful review of the investigative reports in this matter, and based upon the information currently available to this Department, we have concluded that this matter should be closed and that no further action is warranted.

Sincerely,

Albert N. Moskowitz
Section Chief
Criminal Section
Civil Rights Division

U.S. Department of Justice letter exonerating Detective Thomas Augustine regarding allegations that he violated the civil rights of suspect Herbert Haak. (*Courtesy of Tom Augustine*)

Driver Detail   *PA Department of Transportation*

Driver Demographics   *Source: PennDOT IMS*

AMBROSE;JR, FRED JOHN   15 635 570   06/01/1952
Driver Name   Driver License Number   Date of Birth

M   72   **(BL) BLUE**
Gender   Height (inches)   Eye Color

143 HEDGEROW LN
WEST CHESTER, PA 19380   Driver History
Driver Address

Driver License   *Source: PennDOT IMS*

03/31/2000   06/02/2004   00   **(C) SINGLE VEH**
Issue Date   Expiration Date   Duplicate Count   **<= 26,000.**
                        License Class

        (1) CORRECTIVE   Commercial
Endorsements **LENSES.**   Restrictions
        Restrictions

Photo History   *Source: Viisage Corporation Photo Repository*

Photo Record (1 of 2)
Photo Capture Station Information

04/15/2000 01:00:00   **(096) FRAZER / MALVERN**
Photo Date   Location

9621   **30**   200009630@106046
Operator ID   Station   Viisage Control
        ID   ID

Driver Information

15 635 570   06/01/1952
Driver License Number   Date of Birth

CHESTER
County

DRIVER'S LICENSE   **YES**
License Card Type   Organ Donor

PA Department of Transportation info sheet on John Fred Ambrose, Jr., the attorney who masterminded the case accusing John Lambert with the murder of Kimberly Ernest. (*Courtesy of Tom Augustine*)

Personal proclamation to the detectives of the Homicide Division of the Police Department of the City of Philadelphia from Pope John Paul II. (*Courtesy of Tom Augustine*)

To the Detectives of the Homicide Division of the Police Department of the City of Philadelphia, as a sign of my concern for their spiritual welfare and with confidence in God's special care for "America's Unknown Child," I willingly impart my Apostolic Blessing.

From the Vatican, March 15, 1999

Joannes Paulus II

Philadelphia Inquirer article, August 16, 2002, reporting the award of a $40.8 million defamation lawsuit to the parents of John Lambert. (*Courtesy of Tom Augustine*)

$40.8 million awarded in defamation lawsuit

The parents of John Lambert said lawyers falsely accused their son in a rape-murder case.

ASSOCIATED PRESS

A couple who contended their now-deceased son was falsely accused of a sensational Philadelphia murder have won a $40.8 million defamation verdict in Common Pleas Court.

A jury granted the award — $8.5 million in compensatory damages and more than $32 million in punitive damages — to Jay and Barbara Lambert.

The Lamberts had filed suit in 1999 accusing two lawyers and three other men of falsely blaming their son, John, for the 1995 murder of Kimberly Ernest in what was known as the "Center City jogger" case. John Lambert, who filed the original defamation lawsuit, died of a heroin overdose at age 27 on Feb. 1, 1999.

The lawyers held liable in the verdict are Fred Ambrose, who disappeared in April 2001, and Samuel Malat. The other defendants were two investigators, Stephen Stouffer and Albert Tyree, and Leonard Wise.

Common Pleas Court Judge Alan Tereshko, who presided at a trial that began Monday, ruled that Ambrose, Malat and other defendants had defamed John Lambert and ordered the eight-member jury to decide damages.

Mark B. Sheppard, attorney for the Lamberts, said that the directed verdict came after the judge had barred the defendants from putting on a defense. He said the judge took that action because the defendants had repeatedly refused to turn over material the Lamberts sought in pretrial discovery proceedings.

The jury rendered its $40.8 million verdict, which included $21 million in punitive damages against Ambrose and $11 million against Malat, on Wednesday. Other defendants were ordered to pay a total of $275,000 in punitive damages. The $8.5 million compensatory award was levied against all five defendants.

Malat and Ambrose had filed civil lawsuits against the city on behalf of two men who were tried in Ernest's murder in 1997 and acquitted. The acquitted men, Richard Wise, son of Leonard Wise, and Herbert Haak, claimed in their lawsuits that Philadelphia detectives had used violence and false confessions to "maliciously prosecute" them.

To bolster Wise's chances of winning his suit, the Lamberts claimed, Ambrose identified John Lambert as Ernest's likely killer and suggested that Haak and Wise had been framed. Wise's father also was accused of circulating defamatory information about John Lambert.

Ambrose claimed there was a conspiracy to protect John Lambert because Jay Lambert was a partner at the prominent law firm of Duane Morris where Marjorie O. Rendell, now a federal judge, once worked. Rendell's husband is former Mayor Ed Rendell, the Democratic candidate for governor of Pennsylvania.

"Lawyers can be zealous, but they can't malign whomever they want ... in an effort to prevail on behalf of a client," said Sheppard, who is also a Duane Morris partner. Sheppard said his clients would attempt to collect the judgment.

"The case really wasn't about money. The case was about vindicating my partner and his son," Sheppard said.

He said that Duane Morris was picking up the tab for prosecuting the case.

Ambrose disappeared last year, just before he was to give a deposition in the Lamberts' suit. He did not attend the trial. Malat could not be reached for comment yesterday.

Ernest, 26, was a paralegal who was beaten, raped and strangled while on her morning jog through a downtown neighborhood. Her body was left in an outside stairwell. No one has been convicted in her death.

PHILADELPHIA DAILY NEWS   THURSDAY, MARCH 22, 2001

Judge doesn't buy defense

Herbert Haak tried to use tactic that cleared him in 1995 jogger killing; he's convicted of fraud

by Dave Racher

Daily News Staff Writer

There was only one spectator for most of Herbert Haak's check-fraud trial this week.

Sitting in the third row was veteran homicide Detective Thomas Augustine, who was awaiting a call to testify at a murder trial in a nearby room.

Augustine was the detective who once testified he took a confession from Haak to the 1995 rape and murder of Center City jogger Kimberly Ernest.

Haak, 31, claimed the confession had been coerced and accused Augustine of framing him.

A jury bought the story and acquitted Haak and co-defendant Richard Wise in 1997.

Police called the verdict a travesty.

"I just wanted him to see my face," said Augustine, who sat quietly during the two-day case.

After noticing Augustine in the courtroom, Haak glanced over his shoulder a few times, then turned back quickly when he realized the detective was still present.

An investigation by the U.S. Justice Department found no evidence that Haak or Wise had been abused during their questioning, clearing Augustine and Sgt. Paul Musi.

But Haak and Wise still have a civil suit pending against the detectives and the city.

Defense attorney Fred Ambrose decided to use Augustine's presence to try to win an acquittal for Haak in the check case.

He accused Augustine and police of framing Haak. Augustine, who had nothing to do with probing the facts of the case on trial, maintained his cool.

Common Pleas Judge Gary S. Glazer didn't buy the argument.

He convicted Haak, formerly of Northeast Philadelphia, of theft and of passing a bad check. Haak was cleared of forgery and theft by deception. Sentencing was deferred. Haak could get up to 12 years for the crime.

Assistant District Attorney Sandjai Weaver said Haak passed a worthless $6,465 check on Sept. 10, 1999, while buying equipment at a Somerton computer store.

Weaver said Haak went into the store in the Somerton Shopping Center on Bustleton Avenue and bought four personal computers and a laptop, and paid with a phony check.

Police say the check was out of a nonexisting account.

At the time, Haak was operating a computer sales company.

Haak is serving 15 to 30 years in jail for his role in the robbery and beating of a gay man three days before Ernest's body was found in a stairwell at 21st and Pine streets. ■

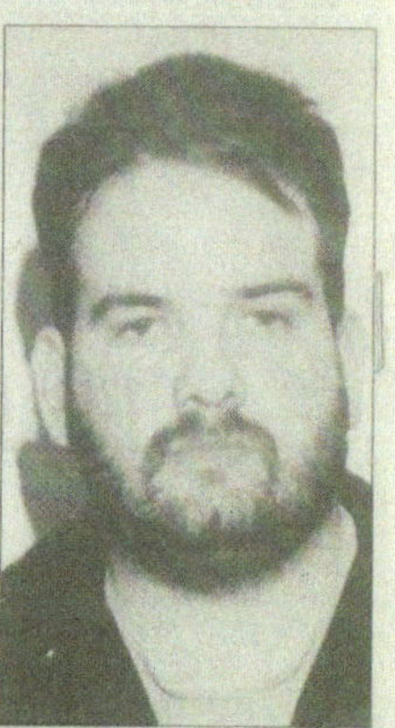

Herbert Haak was acquitted in '95 murder by claiming coercion.

Philadelphia Daily News headline, March 2001, Herbert Haak convicted of fraud. (*Courtesy of Tom Augustine*)

New 'suspect' in jogger case?

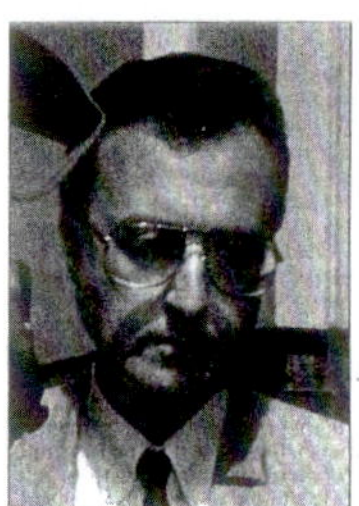

JIM MacMILLAN/ DAILY NEWS
Fred Ambrose: Cites informants

by Joseph R. Daughen

Daily News Staff Writer

A lawyer who is suing the city for false arrest on behalf of one of the defendants acquitted in the murder of jogger Kimberly Ernest said yesterday that he has identified a "prime suspect" in the case.

Fred J. Ambrose, who represents Herbert Haak, made his announcement in a theatrical appearance in a Criminal Justice Center courtroom just as Judge D. Webster Keogh was about to sentence the alleged "prime suspect" for a probation violation unrelated to the Ernest case.

Ambrose said he came to court to offer evidence that he said the judge should know about his alleged suspect. Speaking in court, he said his own eight-month investiga-

Haak's lawyer says own investigation uncovered 'evidence'

tion of the case brought to light the identity of the "suspect." But after leaving the courtroom, Ambrose refused to repeat his accusation.

Under examination by defense attorney John Griffin, Ambrose testified that no state or federal officials had told him that they considered the man he identified to be a suspect. Ambrose said he had his own "criminal and confidential informants," whom he refused to name. He denied that he had anonymously faxed a three-page document to the judge that tried to link Griffin's client to the 1995 Ernest

murder.

Griffin told reporters that his client has never been questioned about the murder by police, and he characterized Ambrose's accusation as "absurd." His client was identified in court as John Lambert, 27, of 15th Street near Jackson.

Griffin also dismissed Ambrose's accusation as a "stunt" designed to call attention to the suit he has filed for Haak, who, along with Richard Wise, was found not guilty of the murder.

Assistant District Attorney Theresa Krause, the prosecutor in Lambert's case, told Keogh the government "has no verification of anything" Ambrose said.

Law enforcement sources consistently have said they believe that Haak and Wise, not anyone else, killed Ernest. ■

JIM MacMILLAN/ DAILY NEWS
John Griffin: Dismisses "stunt"

Philadelphia Daily News article, June 17, 1998, announcing a new suspect in the Center City jogger case. (*Courtesy of Tom Augustine*)

care if he made any money from the case, "not a cent," as he said, especially considering how the future would unravel when he would disappear from view with his clients' money. The religious-like fervor that seemed to motivate him in finding Kimberly's "real" killer certainly put him on a pedestal of sorts, a spiritual plateau high above all those other scummy lawyers whose only interest was money. He was presenting himself as a truth seeker, a risk taker with saintly attributes, a Mother Teresa among lawyers.

The good and just lawyer fighting an evil city whose police detectives forced Haak and Wise to sign forced confessions. This perversion of the good struck me as even more of a sin when I discovered years later that this same Fred Ambrose had at one time thought of entering the priesthood. The priesthood? What kind of priest, I wondered. A friar? A Trappist monk like Thomas Merton? A diocesan priest with a big car who dips into the parish funds?

Ambrose finished his comment by stating how rough the case must have been on Kimberly's mother, Dorothe.

"I'd like to ask you," I said, "Why Kimberly's mother isn't supporting you. Why is she so withdrawn? Is it because you're tied in with Haak and she believes that Haak was one of the murderers and she just can't get past that?"

I was really beginning to believe Ambrose by now. His soliloquy about not caring if he made a cent had done its brainwashing work on me. I could not understand why the City was not listening to this good man. Here he was in his little law firm in Bala Cynwyd while his mighty enemies like Jay Lambert savored spectacular views of the city in their skyscraper suites in One Liberty Place. Ambrose was a Robin Hood in aviator glasses.

I resolved then and there to help him as much as I could, at least to try to get my *Au Courant* editors to document his struggle against the city and a powerful attorney.

"I think there was a lot going on with Mrs. Ernest at the time," Ambrose said. "I find it very hard to believe that she is not even curious enough to look further into this. And I find that very interesting. I really can't tell you anything more beyond that at this point.... But, I find it interesting that she being an educated woman—she is a psychotherapist in Chicago—doesn't have the curiosity, the minimum curiosity to even question this whole thing in light of the information we've been able to uncover. So I find that extreme. Why, I don't know, but I will find out..."

I asked about Kimberly's aunt, Sandra Brewer, an assistant district attorney in Los Angeles, who had been cooperating with Ambrose. "She's been giving us some background information on Kimberly, and unlike the mother she has shown a lot more curiosity about this thing and is reacting the way you would expect anybody to react to these questions..."

I had seen Dorothe Ernest's picture in the news, and knew that she had come to the city several times to sort out the details of her daughter's death. She appeared to be a smart, dignified woman with an extraordinary amount of composure. I had heard that she met with Mayor Rendell and that she was separated from her husband, but beyond that I did not know much about her.

I asked Ambrose if Billy had come forward and accused John of the murder.

"Did you see the videotape that the TV ran?" Ambrose asked. "Well, we took a videotape of Billy several months ago and somehow it got leaked to the press and they ran edited portions of it. On the tape he says that he saw Lambert with Kimberly. He was with John at 17th and Pine when he saw John encounter Kimberly, saw an altercation begin there and saw John grab her and certain things occur on the morning of the murder..."

I did not ask Ambrose to explain what those "certain things" were because I assumed it referred to more fighting. "Do you know the extent of Billy's involvement?"

"Our understanding is that Billy hung out quite a bit with John, both in the street and in his apartment."

"Why wouldn't the City be interested in the information you have? It all sounds pretty powerful. They could at least sit down with you and try to be objective. What's the problem?"

"The problem is the backlash of this whole thing," Ambrose said:

Like I said in the beginning, if they reopen the case they are going to raise doubts about the confession which raises serious questions about police misconduct.

Any criminal investigation will tell you that if they reopen the case they are saying there's still a killer out there. So far the official position is that they've got the killers, Haak and Wise. The jury let them off. If they reopen the case they are backing off from that position. Why reopen the case if you believe you have the killers?

So that's the first problem the City is trying to build. The second problem is the scandal that might come to light—the possible cover-up and the people involved in the cover-up and that sort of thing. So there are a lot of disadvantages to reopening this case. But they are going to have to do it eventually...

I asked Ambrose when he was going to call a press conference to announce his findings. He told me he was taking it day by day, but it could happen at any moment. He added that John Lambert was in custody in the City on some other charges having to do with probation violations but that he will soon be sentenced on drug charges.

"That's going to happen over the next month," he said. "And he'll at least be in jail for a minimum of nine months. We found out through our sources that he had been let out of custody before to go into a rehab but then we came across information that led us to believe that he would flee the area. He's afraid of possible charges of homicide on the Ernest case. He would set certain plans into play that would get him out of the country."

This was serious stuff, indeed.

John Lambert fleeing the country like Philadelphia's notorious Ira Einhorn after Einhorn was charged with the murder of Holly Maddux in Powelton Village. I had to wonder: would Lambert's powerful father, the lawyer on the top floor of Liberty Place, be helping him escape? Would John take Billy with him as his favorite court jester and side kick? I imagined Lambert and Billy in France both wearing berets and haunting the cafes in search of various drugs and murdering women on the side.

The fact that I had quite possibly entertained a killer in my apartment was unnerving.

Because of what Ambrose was telling me, I reexamined Lambert's body language when I was with him. Was the reason that he always seemed so controlled because he had to put a tight rein on his otherwise monstrous emotions? I wondered how close I had come to witnessing Lambert lashing out when he was with Stuart and me. What could set somebody like this off—a word, gesture, facial grimace, a perceived attitude? Ambrose's contention that there was something to Lambert's lingering by my kitchen window and looking out at the stairwell—something more than an observer's curiosity as if Lambert was revisiting the scene of the crime in his mind, reliving the horror of it all—now made sense to me.

"We brought this to the attention of the court at that time and instead of putting him in rehab they put him in jail for nine months so he's sitting in jail right now in safe keeping," Ambrose said. In safe keeping, like jewelry in a safe deposit box.

Ambrose told me he made several attempts to visit John in jail but that each time John refused to see him. "He doesn't even protest his innocence in this whole thing, and he is very, very worried about what is going to happen to him."

He talked about Lambert's intelligence and his good sense in listening to his lawyer who told him not say anything. Ambrose understood why Lambert wasn't talking to him.

I asked Ambrose if he thought that Kimberly was raped in the stairwell.

"The Philadelphia coroner, a Dr. Preston, stands by his opinion that the semen found in Ernest's body was from the attackers. In fact, if you look at the trial transcript, the DA put Dr. Preston on the stand as part of the City's case and Dr.

Preston stated to Assistant DA Judi Rubino that this was the case. Rubino acted surprised by that testimony and then later she shopped around for another coroner, and he tried to present testimony that it was consensual sex from the night before. He was cross-examined and he broke down, and then they brought another medical examiner who corroborated Dr. Preston's testimony. So, yes, I think it's a fact that she was sexually molested by her attacker, and the jury decided the case based on that issue. The DNA did not match Haak and Wise."

I asked if there was going to be a DNA test on John Lambert.

"I would love to do so. I've been demanding, I've been requesting, I've been asking. I've been pleading for it both from his family members, from the City, from anybody who would listen to me but nobody has offered it to me or given me the opportunity to get his DNA."

"If somebody is innocent one sure way to prove it is to give me a DNA. Give it to me. If it doesn't match that sperm, I'll forget John Lambert, I'll forget that he even exists. I've spoken to his father about the DNA. I've spoken to his lawyer about it, and I've spoken to John's mother as well. And absolutely nothing."

"About John's past: Skip Thomas told me that John almost beat his sister's brains in or something like that, so he does have a checkered past," I said.

"Yeah, we found this out from his mother. His mother told us that and that was covered up also. Apparently he beat her so badly that she had permanent brain damage. There are problems, neurological problems..."

"That's a lot more than sibling rivalry," I said.

"Way beyond that.... Apparently he used a baseball bat on her because she caught him trying to steal some of her jewelry or something in the house. He beat her up.... Tell me," Ambrose added, "Are you going to some day write a book about this, or an article?"

"I don't know where anything is going from here," I said. "It may be an article."

Ambrose walked around the office. "For anybody who looked at this case very quickly sees the inconsistencies and sees that there is something drastically wrong with the official version."

"I can tell you that on that day, November 2nd, I knew it wasn't a homeless man at the bottom of the stairwell because of the way that the police, the detectives and the EMT people were almost leering when they looked down there. It occurred to me then that it was an unclothed or partially clothed woman. You could tell it was a woman by the way the men were looking down there. It's as if they couldn't help it, human nature, that sort of thing..."

"Let me show you a picture of a police officer. I want to see if you recognize him," Ambrose said, taking a photograph out of a folder. "I think this may be one of the police officers that interviewed you, but I'm not sure."

"He looks like an SS officer from WWII," I said. "No, I don't remember him."

"How about this guy?"

"Maybe him," I said. "There is something familiar about him, but..."

"How about the officers that harassed you that one night?" Ambrose asked. "Did either one of them look like that?" Ambrose was referring to the uniformed officers who stopped me on Pine Street as I was walking and talking with a 17th and Pine habitué.

"Those officers ... one was tall with wide aviator glasses and light hair. The other one was short, stocky, Italian, dark hair."

"Both uniformed police officers?"

"Yes, of course. Oddly enough, I think I had them back when I was doing an article for *City Paper*. I interviewed them both in my apartment for a piece I was doing on male prostitutes and they came over on their bikes. We all parted friends. It was all very weird.... Only in Philadelphia."

"Did they give you any reason why they hassled you that day?"

"Immediately after the incident, I called Captain Tianno of the 9th District and I complained to him, and then wrote him a letter, you know. He apologized on behalf of the officers and so as far as I was concerned it was a done deal."

Ambrose took out another folder and withdrew a small photograph. "This guy here, does his face look familiar to you?"

"Yes it does."

'Where did they interview you, down at police headquarters?"

"It was at the Roundhouse at Eighth and Race, the Police Municipal Building. At the time the idea was—this is what the detective told me—that she had been killed in the stairwell, that her face had been bashed against the brick wall in the stairwell. That was the consensus then, that she was killed in the stairwell and that she had been raped or sodomized in the stairwell. Then the story came back and it was all revised, edited and changed. I don't know what new evidence they found to make those changes."

"That's why I mentioned to you a while ago that I think the investigation was proceeding along normally up until mid-November. Obviously the police interviewed you around that time, right?"

"I was interviewed the same day that she was killed," I said.

"They were doing a good job investigating this case up to mid-November, then something changed," Ambrose said.

"One scenario they came up with is that they saw her running and then forced her in their car and rode her around town," I offered.

"The official scenario that was presented at the trial was that Haak and Wise were out trying to steal cars around 18th and Spruce."

"18th and Pine," I interjected.

"I think Spruce came up too a couple of times, and she came jogging along and she encountered Richie Wise, and then Richie whacked her with a tire iron, threw her in a car that Haak had and raped her in the car, then killed her in the car. That was the official story presented at the trial. And then they drove around trying to find a place to put the body."

"Killed her in the car on the spot, not as they were driving the car," I offered.

"A combination of the two," Ambrose said. "He got her into the car and as Haak was driving along he finished her off in the car. That was the official story. And then they went to find some place to dump the body and they found a stairwell at 21st and Pine. So the official story is that she was killed elsewhere in a car?"

"Yes."

"Not in the stairwell?"

I agreed.

"Well, this is clearly inconsistent with all the other evidence in the case. That's all. Any other questions I can answer as well."

"I think I'm okay," I told Ambrose. "But, could you give me your ending to this story."

"My ending is that John Lambert will be charged with murder, or at least this case will be reopened and he'll be brought in for questioning. I think it will be more beyond that. I think it's going to take many months. The first step, of course is getting John brought up on the charge. And I think once that's done the final scientific tests will be done and used in court and that clinches who did it. But there's going to be a lot more beyond that, and I'll be in the audience with you. You know," Ambrose continued, "I wanted to be a writer myself but never had the gumption or the time to sit down and actually write something and in fact I don't even have the talent. If you can sell it, if you can write books and they sell and you can make a living off of it, which I understand is very hard..."

"The rewards are great, Fred, but there's a lot of loneliness, self-discipline and personal sacrifice involved, but I don't think I would trade it for anything..."

"You know," Ambrose added, "I'm still reading that science fiction book you gave me and from what I've read so far you're very, very good..."

"Thank you," I said. "That's the same book I gave to John Lambert."

"You caught me interest right off the bat with it. You said it was the worst of your books..."

"One of my least successful ones. I think that book should have had a better editor because there are too many typos."

"I caught some," Ambrose said. "The word *assertation* is in there instead of assertion."

"It's not a perfect book but it is what it is," I said.

"I'll be watching the newsstands and the bookstores for your name in future years. Maybe when this case is over there will be some more material for you to write a novel on."

"I can't get away from this case. It keeps following me around. When I think I've put it behind me the phone rings and it's somebody else connected with it."

"Look Thom," Ambrose said, leaning towards me. "After Steve first spoke with you, did anybody contact you after that? You know, like any private individuals, anything like that?"

Other than my neighbor Allen and a few friends, and, of course, Chuck, nobody was asking or prying into my life. "Should I feel nervous about something?"

"Well, there have been occasions where we've spoken to people and then others who want to find out what we know will question the same people we questioned to get a feel for what we're talking about. I was just curious if somebody may have approached you after we spoke with you."

"It's been extremely quiet. I don't even think anybody knows that I'm being questioned except for a few friends. That's it."

I stood up, we shook hands and then I took the bus back to Center City. Allen was in the vestibule of the apartment building when I returned and I told him that I had come from Bala Cynwyd where I had an interview with a lawyer who was charging somebody else with the murder of Kimberly Ernest.

"Who?" Allen asked.

"A guy named John Lambert. He's been here a few times; you may have seen him, a tall guy with a long ponytail." Allen told me he did not recall anybody like that, although he was always commenting on the handsome men who were visiting me as he had a large peephole in his apartment door.

7

WHEN PRIVATE INVESTIGATORS THINK THEY'RE THE FBI

Very soon I would discover why Lambert did not want anything to do with Ambrose. The entire time Ambrose's law firm was counting me as one of its front-line journalists ("We'll fill you in on the day to day details if you make yourself available to us for questioning"), they were planning something else.

A week after my last trip to Bala Cynwyd, I received a call from Ambrose's office asking me if I would come to the office right away. I was told that something important had happened with the case. Ambrose was so eager to see me he said that he would have Skip Thomas chauffeur me from another appointment I had earlier in the day in Sharon Hill, Pennsylvania.

Important? Had they discovered another suspect other than John Lambert? Mr. Fineman, the dog walker, who discovered the body, the Peeping Tom, Chuck, or one of my neighbors? Had John Lambert confessed to the murder?

I knew things were bad the moment I entered Ambrose's office. Call it a vibe, a premonition. Ambrose tried to be charming, but the ruse crumbled shortly thereafter when he told me he was convinced that I was hiding something I had seen on the morning of the murder.

There was not much left to say. I told Ambrose how disappointed I was in him, after which he directed Skip Thomas to drive me back to the city. Thomas and I barely spoke during the tense fifteen-minute drive on the Schuylkill expressway.

A day later, on a Saturday, my door buzzer rang. The visitors announced themselves as Stephen Stouffer and Skip Thomas. When I buzzed them inside, they came running up the staircase and entered my apartment in the crudest way imaginable—without saying hello or waiting to being invited to sit down. The visit was more like a raid.

Without hesitation, both men laid into me: You're hiding something; we think you know who murdered Kimberly Ernest; we even think you may be an accomplice of some sort. They spoke of consequences if I did not tell them what I was hiding. I told them that I knew nothing more than what I had already revealed and that they would have to accept that. Stouffer's behavior was especially troubling, so troubling in fact that I prepared myself for violence.

Would that happen? I was not sure, but very negative energy was in the room. They spoke of consequences (again) if I did not "own up" and added that this was my last chance to come clean. I told them that this behavior indicated to me that the Ambrose team and their investigation was a total fraud. I suggested that they leave the apartment. As they walked towards the door, I was careful to keep a safe distance from Stouffer. Men of his type are quick to act. I was afraid he would throw a punch or two.

The two of them raced down the staircase and out the front door. I looked at them on the street from my kitchen window and watched as they entered a car and drove away as a female jogger—a power walker—shuttled past the stairwell.

I was upset but also angry and called the Ambrose firm and left a scolding message on the voicemail. Then I called the City, the police, and a detective who had given me his number and left a message asking him to call me back. I was calling everybody. Going to extremes they call it, but something had to be done.

I wondered if Stouffer would return at a later date, perhaps finding a way to enter my apartment without a key, and wait for my arrival and then do God knows what. This seemed entirely possible given the shrewd trickery the Ambrose people had exhibited so far.

The next few days were tense; I kept an eye out for Stouffer whenever I walked through the neighborhood. I was also careful to enter my apartment slowly and keep the door open until I was sure nobody was waiting for me inside. Fortunately, neither Stouffer nor Thomas returned, and Ambrose did not call back.

Then I got a call from *Philadelphia City Paper*. They wanted to send out a reporter and a photographer to get my take on the charges being leveled against John Lambert. By this time, *Au Courant* had had enough of the case and was on to other feature stories.

A *City Paper* photographer came to my apartment and photographed me by my kitchen window looking out at the stairwell. I was becoming a Kimberly Ernest murder celebrity. The feature article by Howard Altman ("The Kimberly Conundrum," CP, January 14, 1999) included a section entitled "A Journalist Threatened."

Ambrose and Stouffer have been a nuisance, too, to Thom Nickels, [that section began]. Nickels lives across the street from where Ernest's body was dumped. A freelance journalist, Nickels wrote a piece about Ambrose's theory—that Lambert killed Ernest—for *Au Courant*, one of the city's two gay weeklies. Nickels says that because Lambert was not charged with the Ernest killing he didn't name Lambert, instead using the name, John Doe.

Appearing in the August 11-17-1998 [*Au Courant*] issue, the story quotes Ambrose as being certain that "John Doe" killed Ernest.

Altman wrote how Ambrose had told him that Saundra Brewer, Kim's aunt, was cooperating with the Ambrose team.

A few paragraphs later, Nickels' Au Courant story takes a very strange turn.

Ambrose said he had evidence that a friend of this John Doe, after Ernest was killed, glanced up and noticed people in a nearby apartment looking down at him.

One of these people was Nickels, who wrote that he saw "nothing but leaves" outside his window.

Since that story came out, Nickels has filed a complaint with the District Attorney's office that two investigators for Fred Ambrose—Stephen Stouffer and Skip Thomas—tried to intimidate him into saying that he did see something out his window on the morning Ernest was killed.

Nickels says his first contact with Stouffer came because he had given a statement to police the morning Ernest was killed and later wrote an opinion piece for the Daily News about the killing. Stouffer was looking for information and was initially polite, Nickels says.

Nickels told Stouffer that John Lambert "was somebody my lover had coffee with and invited up to the apartment. He was somebody we both knew."

Ambrose's investigators, says Nickels, continued to call seeking further information. Nickels says he complied.

Then, in the summer of 1998, Nickels says he decided to write a story about Ambrose's theories on the Ernest killing for *Au Courant*.

Shortly after that story appeared, Nickels' relationship with Ambrose and his team took a turn for the worse, when Nickels says he was called into Ambrose's Bala Cynwyd office to answer some questions.

"This is when they accused me of withholding evidence," Nickels says. "They claimed reliable, unnamed sources saw me talking with Lambert the morning of the murder. I was really outraged by this. That ended the relationship. My integrity as a journalist and a writer were being threatened."

It didn't end there.

In September, Nickels says he was dropped off at his house by his lover only to find Stephen Stouffer waiting. Stouffer, he says, offered to carry his bags upstairs. He profusely apologized for Ambrose's behavior.

In early November, Stouffer appeared at Nickels' apartment again. With a much different attitude.

"Skip Thomas and Stephen Stouffer came running up my stairs and said they had to talk to me," says Nickels. "They just stormed in, looking very desperate. They came in as if they owned the place. They told me that they believed I was withholding information. Stephen Syouffer asked me if I hung out with Kimberly Ernest as the Westbury. The inference was that I was lying and that I knew Ernest. Skip just said he wishes he could believe me."

The conversation, says Nickels, was heated. "Loud enough so that my neighbors could hear."

Nickels says the investigators left after he refused their request to take a polygraph. Then he contacted the DA to file a complaint.

Nickels says that Ambrose and Stouffer changed his mind about the Kimberly Ernest murder.

"In the soul of my soul, I really believed that Lambert did it," says Nickels. "Now, I don't put much faith into that story that Ambrose puts out. If only because of what was done to me."

Stouffer has denied harassing Nickels, saying that Nickels is the one not telling the truth. Thomas has been unavailable for comment.

Ambrose says he has "reliable evidence from other investigators who have been looking into this case that Mr. Nickels saw more than he is telling us."

Nickels should "file a complaint against me," says Ambrose. "I am the one who interrogated him" about allegations that Nickels is withholding evidence.

When I began this book late in 2021, I had all but forgotten about Ambrose's request that I take a polygraph.

At the time I recall feeling quite resentful that Ambrose did not believe me, especially after I went overboard in meeting all of his requests for interviews. But after his series of tricky maneuvers, I came to the conclusion that taking a polygraph would acknowledge that Ambrose's investigation was a legitimate one. It would be seen as an acknowledgment of his credibility. My not wanting to take a polygraph had nothing to do with something to hide, as probably some would suspect. Before my experience with Ambrose I would have been of the same opinion: that refusal to take a polygraph suggested some sort of guilt.

His use of the word "interrogation" to describe our interviews also struck me as significant. While I felt under the gun and at times great annoyance at Ambrose's constant repetition of questions—a Psych One methodology to trick the interviewee—I always felt free to end whatever discussion was taking place and walk out the door.

Nothing was holding me back except the hope, however dim, of latching onto a greater story or some unexpected revelation. That was why I took Ambrose's repetitive hammer blows with relative malleability. Some might call this foolish, but it was something I felt I had to do.

At certain points during Ambrose's interrogation, I felt an extraordinary passion in him for me to give him any sort of answer, however ludicrous, that would fit what by now had become the "Ambrose Narrative."

The boring repetition of telling him what I had seen and experienced can at a certain point appear like a request to lie, exaggerate, and create another thread of drama, just to give the interrogator what he so obviously desperately longed for.

I sensed a hunger in Ambrose's eyes, a real plea for me to exaggerate, to lie, which would then, perhaps, catapult his case against John Lambert into believable realms. Had I lied and stated that I saw John Lambert dispose of the body, what "power" would that have given me over the lives of others?

Had I told Ambrose that I spotted Chuck, my blond accountant friend, arguing with Kimberly on the corner of 21st and Pine and then witnessed him killing her in his white shirt and tie, would he have believed me? Could I have told him anything?

John Lambert was an addict but he hid it well. He was not an addict like Billy Liberatore, wild and untamed and always creating drama in the streets.

Howard Altman, in "The Kimberly Conundrum, Part II" in *Philadelphia City Paper*, writes that "The story of Billy Liberatore, star witness, begins in the swirling vortex of weirdness kicked up by Kimberly Ernest's brutal death."

Altman relates how Richie Wise's father, Len Wise, was faced with so many reporters after his son was arrested that he felt he had to hide out at the shore. Almost immediately, however, Wise was informed by a family member that "a guy named Billy had some dirt on the murder."

"I was contacted by Billy Liberatore the day after my son was arrested," Wise told Altman. "He said a guy named Mike did it." How many "Mikes" do you suppose live in Philadelphia and its suburbs?

Altman then describes how Wise began to unravel the mystery of the guy named Mike.

There was a shooting on Christmas Day 1995 at 1706A Delancey Street, not far from the stairwell at 21st and Pine. The address apparently was known to

Philadelphia Police because it became the subject of an investigation during the hunt for Ernest's killer. The basement apartment at 1706A Delancey was where Liberatore and Mike lived. Len Wise, acting as a private detective, went to the apartment and, according to Altman, talked to the owner, Marty Bergen, who told him that the name on the lease was John Lambert.

In March 1996, *Philadelphia Magazine* published a story titled "The Vampires of Delancey Street," detailing the exploits of a number of crack-addicted male prostitutes around 17th and Pine. The article's "star" character is none other than "Johnny D," or John Lambert. The writer of the piece, Eric Konigsberg, describes Johnny D. as "tall and wisp-waisted, with beady, deep-set eyes, flower-like skin and lank hair bound into a ponytail with a purple scrunchy."

Len Wise, acting on this information—including the shooting that occurred at the apartment on Christmas Day 1995—concluded that John Lambert was the man behind the two identities "Mike" and "Johnny D," and that Lambert was the real killer of Ernest.

In yet another twist, Altman reports that in late February 1996, "an anonymous, handwritten letter, in a plain white envelope, arrived in the hands of Channel 10 WCAU-TV reporter John Blunt."

The letter read:

The killer of Kimberly Ernest is a guy named Mike he lived with a guy named John Lambert at 1706A Delancey Street John and Mike sold Drugs at Delancey Street and 17th and Spruce Street. Mike is tall and about 180lbs. and has long dark hair. On the morning of Nov. 2nd he tried to rape a girl named Michele at that apartment, but John made him go because he was drugged up and crazy. He was seen at 20th and Pine about 3:00 a.m. that morning with a short guy with black hair. Homicide detectives were looking for him on Nov. 4 but could not find him. They were asking about him at 17th and Spruce and gave up. This guy Mike is a bad Dude. I can not give you my name because this guy would Kill me. If he found out....

Please look in to this before he Kills again. Mike is the Killer so why did the police stop looking for him?

Something is wrong with the police. The paper said Kimberly had black and brown hair in her hands. Ask about him on Spruce Street and Pine Street.

Help Stop him.

The police won't. Something is wrong.

Thank you.

When I read this "anonymous letter," my thoughts immediately went to the tall man with long hair I spotted the last time I saw John Lambert alive. The stranger was sitting in a parked car, but I could see that he was practicality Lambert's double. I encountered this situation just as I had turned the corner onto Delancey Street. Lambert gave me a nod then walked over to the car from the stoop where he had been sitting, presumably to take a ride with his doppelgänger. Billy was standing near the stoop, but he did not get into the car. The entire episode lasted only a few seconds, but it was enough for me to get a good look at the driver, the man that Billy later told me was Lambert's brother and his main drug connection.

Perhaps this man was the so-called dangerous "Mike" referred to in the anonymous letter. While closely resembling Lambert, the man seemed to have a thicker-looking build. He was tall but hardly "wisp-waisted, with beady, deep-set eyes, flower-like skin and lank hair bound into a ponytail with a purple scrunchy." I wrote earlier about how I felt that I was seeing double when I first laid eyes on him.

Altman reported that Blunt turned the letter over to the police on the very day it was reported that the DNA evidence found on Ernest did not match Haak or Wise:

> The letter came at a very bad time for Judi Rubino, the brash blonde assistant district attorney who saw the Ernest case blow up in her hands; first with the unhelpful DNA analysis and then with statements from Haak and Wise that they were beaten into signing blank papers.
>
> Presented with the kind of juicy morsel that is rarely seen and never passed up, the media had a predictable feast, roasting Rubino as the sacrificial pig.
>
> It was the talk of the town.

Then the most astounding event occurred:

> On March 27, 1996, in the wake of the DNA bomb, Billy Liberatore stepped out of the shadows and put his name to a statement distributed by Len Wise and Stephen Stouffer about what took place the morning Kimberly was killed.

The same Stephen Stouffer who raided my apartment and tried to bully me into confessing something I never saw. The same Stephen Stouffer who hung out on my stoop at 21st and Pine in a pair of shorts and a tank top, looking like a street hustler himself, waiting for my arrival so he could bamboozle his way into my apartment. Here also was Len Wise, a man I had never met, the father of a troubled violent homophobe who walked the streets of Center City half naked in the summer just to attract the attention of gay men so he could turn around and attack them.

The Kimberly Ernest gospel, according to Billy Liberatore:

After all night of smoking crack cocaine, John D. acting really crazy went upstairs to his room and then left through another door upstairs to go outside.

John D. came back to the house at approximately 6:15 a.m. through another entrance downstairs. He threw crack at me and Michelle (a girl I was with). He was extremely nervous. He was sweaty and his hair was all messed up. He then ran upstairs to the bathroom. After approximately one hour he came back downstairs and he still seemed extremely nervous. He constantly chewed gum. The following day people on the block were saying that John D. had killed the girl (Kimberly Ernest).

I did not see John D. again until two or three days later and I noticed that his hands were scratched and scrapped up.

The reason I have not come forward sooner with this information is because I fear for my life if I say anything about that night.

Billy Liberatore's confession contradicted Ambrose's account of what happened on the morning of November 2, 1995, namely that Liberatore helped Lambert drag Ernest into the stairwell, and that both men spotted me looking at them in the street from my kitchen window. It also contradicted the contents of the anonymous letter delivered to John Blunt that pointed to "Mike" as the real killer of Ernest.

According to the *City Paper* article, a Secret Service-certified typing analyst determined that Liberatore's confession letter and the letters sent to John Blunt and other news sources warning them that a serial killer was responsible for Ernest's death, "contained so many similarities that the combined effect … certainly suggests a singular typist."

Altman ascribes Billy Liberatore as being the author.

There were other things in Altman's piece that interested me. One was his examination of Ambrose's charge that Kimberly Ernest was one in a line of several woman who had been the victim of a serial killer. The serial killer, of course, was John Lambert. One of the women killed by this serial killer, Tammy Pierce, was murdered in April 1996. The twenty-eight-year old Fishtown woman was strangled to death on the railroad tracks that run through Kensington. Her body was later discovered by teens.

Altman interviewed Darlene Delange, Tammy's sister, who was once close friends with John Lambert when the two of them were in the same Roxborough drug treatment center in 1996. Delange revealed to the journalist that Lambert and she were "very close."

Delange recalls Lambert as "a nice-looking guy who all the girls liked," and as someone who spent "hours telling stories about his wild life in Center City that included a fancy apartment, rampant sex and drugs, and even a star turn in *Philadelphia Magazine*."

Delange said: "He would show me a copy of the magazine and tell me it was him. He would tell me all these stories, but I thought he was full of shit." Delange's other comments: "He was so freaking skinny, he couldn't fight his way out of a paper bag;" "I never heard his name in conjunction with my sister's murder;" "I still have his Bible. When he gave it to me, I knew he was never coming back to the rehab center."

Delange also stated that he never mentioned Kimberly Ernest and did not seem to be violent.

In Ambrose's civil action on behalf of Herbert C. P. Haak filed on October 27, 1997, he lists similarities in the seven cold-case serial killer victims in the city from 1995 to 1996:

He states that all seven (7) victims were found or murdered in the early morning hours, all 7 were found in drug areas, all 7 had reddish/brown hair, all 7 had been severely beaten and strangled, all 7 were sexually assaulted, and all 7 had defensive wounds.

The victims:

Kimberly Ernest	11/2/95	21st. and Pine Street
Tammy Pierce	4/14/96	Ruth and Tusculum Streets (railroad tracks)
Nina Marie Borgesi	4/21/96	Randolf and Turner Streets (loading dock)
Trinity Miller	6/16/96	Bristol, PA (vacant lot)
Aimee Willard	6/20/96	16th and Indiana Avenue (vacant lot)
Jane Doe	?/?/?	Trenton and Monmouth St. (abandoned house)
Anje Maldonado	10/2/96	Hope and Montgomery Ave. (abandoned house)

In concluding his summary, Ambrose wrote:

I believe the killer is a white male 6' 2" long brown hair 170 to 180 pounds thin built—he is a heavy crack addict ... his crack addiction is what puts him in the areas of the homicides.

The Philadelphia Police Homicide Unit has his name and never picked him up in any of these homicides. This case needs a federal investigation to solve it—not the Philadelphia Police Homicide Unity—they won't do it.... They do not care about the girls being murdered or the families of the girls being murdered.... Are they trying to hide the real identity of the killer or cover-up for someone?????

In a June 2, 1998 letter to then Mayor Edward G. Rendell, Ambrose introduces himself as representing Herbert Haak in regard to Haak's lawsuit against the city for his arrest and prosecution for the murder of Kimberly Ernest.

He goes on to say that, during the course of his firm's representation of Mr. Haak, "certain disturbing issues have come to light which make it abundantly clear that the original official investigation fell far short of competent and acceptable police investigation."

"At this juncture," he continues, "I am taking the liberty of contacting you by letter in the hope that your office will join us in what has come to be our 'crusade' to rectify the injustices that have been done in this matter."

Ambrose then lists fourteen facts about the case that he hopes will convince the mayor that the murder should be "re-examined."

WINTERGREEN-FLAVORED CHEWING GUM

Number 13 concerns a wad of chewing gum that was discovered in the stairwell near where the body which was, upon examination, determined to have been of Wintergreen flavor and chewed by an individual in the A blood grouping. "Our investigation has indicated that it is very likely that our suspect was chewing gum of this particular flavor the morning of the murder."

In 1995, I chewed a lot of Wintergreen gum and had the nervous habit of putting several sticks in my mouth at once. In those days, I was not always "neighborly" when it came to disposing of gum that no longer had its flavor, so there were occasions when I would discreetly flick a used wad into the bottom of the stairwell in the years preceding the murder (after the murder, the stairwell had come to represent for me a kind of sacred space). It is somewhat likely that the gum came from me, passing the stairwell as often as I did, sometimes up to three or four times a day. I do not recall John Lambert ever chewing gum, although Stuart was a big chewer and his favorite was also Wintergreen.

Ambrose also noted that "According to the autopsy report, it was apparent that she put up a very strenuous defense during her attack. This is inconsistent with Haak or Wise having been involved in this matter since not even a scratch was found on either of their bodies when they were attending a Hearing approximately three hours following the murder in a Bucks County Magistrate Court.".

The Bala Cynwyd attorney also made note that a vehicle parked near the stairwell at 21st and Pine demonstrated evidence of a struggle over the hood and other portions of the vehicle with extensive fingerprints, handprints, and other brush marks on the vehicle. "Not only were no prints able to be lifted from this vehicle but the existence of this vehicle is also inconsistent with the official scenario as to how and where the attack took place."

The vehicle was Mr. Fineman's car, which was usually parked in front of his house and rarely used. In 1995, a day or two after the murder I watched as the police towed it away and then returned it to its regular parking spot in front of the stairwell.

Ambrose also wrote to then Police Commissioner John S. Timoney asking him to re-open the case. "At this juncture, it is imperative that the first step be taken, i.e., the re-opening of this case so that all issues arising in this matter can be appropriately addressed and this matter can, once and for all, be laid to rest along with its victim." Ambrose mentions "collateral" issues that he says will "be quickly addressed and unraveled once the initial re-investigation of the murder itself is initiated."

Ambrose points out to Timoney that the individual suspected of the murder of Ms. Ernest is John Salago Lambert because he fits fairly accurately "the description of a suspect walking away near the scene of the crime on November 2, 1995 as described by two independent witnesses and subsequently reduced by them to a police sketch, which remarkably resembles our suspect."

So, two neighbors of mine were eyewitnesses to the crime and actually saw Lambert walking away from the stairwell in the early morning hours of November 2?

Ambrose claimed to have obtained the sworn statement of an eyewitness who placed the suspect, John Lambert, with the victim, Ms. Ernest, at the location of 17th and Pine Street "within minutes prior to her assault and murder which occurred between 17th and Pine and 21st and Pine, with the victim's body being found in a stairwell at 21st and Pine Street."

"Brown hair found in Ms. Ernest's right hand, upon examination did not belong to either Mr. Haak or Mr. Wise—this leads to the question of who did it belong to?" Ambrose adds: "Hair of undetermined species (neither dog nor cat not human) was found on the victim's body. The forensic examiners of Philadelphia County refer to this hair as belonging to an 'exotic animal' of some type. We have determined through our investigation that our suspect was the owner of various types of 'exotic' animals at the time of this murder."

In a statement that disparages the victim's moral character, Ambrose claims to have spoken with ATF informants that placed "Ms. Ernest (or a female who very closely matches her description) in a drug buy in the Kensington area."

Ambrose makes the case that because Ms. Ernest and Lambert traveled in the same circles and because Lambert was a known drug user and dealer and distributor of drugs on the streets of Philadelphia, that Kimberly Ernest by default was also a drug user.

Anyone who has taken the time to walk through the streets of Kensington, especially near Kensington and Allegheny, will realize that the numbers of women on the streets with reddish brown and blond hair are literally "uncountable."

Women with this hair coloring in fact far outnumber women with brown or black hair. Who knows why this is the case but during my many visits to that area when I was researching my two books on Philadelphia's homeless, I have always noted the high percentage of girls and women with strawberry-blonde hair. This is why the statement, "Ms. Ernest (or a female who very closely matches her description) in a drug buy in the Kensington area" is absolutely ludicrous and illustrates Ambrose's blatant disconnect with reality. It is about as far a stretch as when Ambrose claimed that I spotted Lambert and Liberatore on the morning of November 2, 1995 on Pine Street looking up at my kitchen window.

While Ambrose's letter to Timoney is full of farfetched "stretches," he does raise some interesting questions. One is his contention that Lambert returned to his apartment on the morning of November 2, 1995 "with numerous scratches and marks on his face and hands, not wearing a shirt, and in a very nervous and agitated mental state." Another is his statement that Kimberly Ernest's aunt, Ms. Saundra Brewer, a senior district attorney in Los Angeles County, thought that his request to re-open the case had merit.

In yet another puzzling charge, Ambrose states that among the evidence collected at the scene of the crime was a "Walkman" radio and headset which was found immediately adjacent to the parked vehicle which was covered in fingerprints, handprints, and scruff marks.

The discovery of the "Walkman" was reported in the press so it cannot be relegated to a figment of Ambrose's imagination. Ambrose raises an interesting point when he asks: "This is inconsistent with the official scenario that Haak and Wise abducted Ms. Ernest at a location several blocks from 21st and Pine, molested and attacked her in a vehicle and thereafter transported her to the stairwell at 21st and Pine and disposed of her body."

The assumption that Ambrose is making here is that the "Walkman" would have been lost in transit during the "alleged" attack several blocks from 21st and Pine, even though during a life-and-death struggle something like a Walkman could have become entangled around Ernest's throat or caught in her hair or somehow been wedged or twisted around her arm. Or it could have fallen on the car floor and then when she was dragged out to the stairwell it could have been dragged out of the car with her. She could even have attempted to use the Walkman and radio as an instrument of self-defense. These things are impossible to know.

The discovery of the Walkman by the stairwell was significant for me, however, because the screams that woke me up in the wee hours of November 2 had a sudden "surprise" element to them like the screams you would make if you were suddenly attacked by someone jumping down at you from the branches of a tree as you passed underneath on the sidewalk.

They were definitely "shock screams" rather than the screams of a dying woman being hoisted over the railing of a stairwell, or the screams of two men trying to finish off a dying woman as they prepared to place her at the bottom of the stairwell. They were the deathly screams of someone being attacked.

Ambrose also claimed that an Ernest family member told him that the deceased always wore a black running watch on her left arm while jogging. The watch was not found on her body, however, although it is possible that Kimberly forgot to wear the watch on that particular morning. Ambrose slips into another one of his infamous conjectures when he posits: "Our inquiries with a local jewelry merchant indicate the possibility that our suspect may have pawned a watch the day following the murder."

Ambrose mentions that a close Ernest family member stated that throughout her life, the deceased always wore pink/peach-colored underpants under her jogging shorts/pants.

"These underwear were further described as always being plain, as opposed to the frilly type. An identical female undergarment was discovered at the vacated premises of the suspect by an investigator shortly after the murder on November 2, 1995. Laboratory testing of smears and discharge on this undergarment is presently underway..."

Imagine if a male jogger had been killed and left in the stairwell at 21st and Pine. A handsome, lean runner in his twenties with everything going for him, an athletic marvel of a man and city heartthrob; imagine such a victim and then imagine a legal document that focused on his underwear: his black Calvin Klein jockey shorts or Speedo-style boxers with a banana motif. Imagine one of the male victim's close family members coming forward: "He always wore black Speedos with colorful banana accents while jogging. He wore the same style of underwear since he was a teen. His Speedos were plain; they did not have a crotch padding. He was always focused on bananas."

Ambrose concludes in his letter to Timoney:

It is certainly the intention of my office to assist and not to impede or interfere with the official re-investigation of this matter and it is certainly not our intention to usurp the duties and functions of the law enforcement authorities who bear the responsibility of the investigation of crimes in this country. The fruits of our efforts thus far are available to the appropriate authorities in order to facilitate this matter to a speedy conclusion and avoid unnecessary duplication of effort. It is far worse to hide an oversight than it is to simply admit it, rectify it and move on. Credibility, integrity and honor are certainly best served by this approach.... I am not here, as many of my critics would state, "to chase a case," rather, I am here as a citizen absolutely disgusted and outraged with an injustice that has been perpetrated by individuals whose motives are questionable, to say the least...

The shameful campaign to disparage the victim as a "loose woman" and therefore somehow indirectly deserving of the fate that awaited her assumed a new guise when the media concentrated on Kimberly's diary in which she allegedly listed her boyfriends and then commented on their performance as lovers. As police evidence, perhaps a document such as this was crucial in combing for possible suspects, but in the hands of sensationalistic journalists the diary became something else.

Keeping a journal is usually the mark of intelligence and introspection, and writing about the people in your life, friends or lovers, is often a way to understand them at a deeper level. Anais Nin, the great diarist and writer, wrote about her lovers in her legendary 102-volume diary.

Thomas Merton, the Trappist monk and Catholic writer, confided in his journals details of the love affair he had with a young nurse he met while recuperating from surgery in a Louisville hospital.

French writer Andre Gide confided in his journals his many erotic encounters during his world travels. Andy Warhol in his diaries, published after his death, writes about his sex life. Writer and social critic Paul Goodman's diaries, *Five Years*, followed a similar trajectory. In my own journals, I recorded my encounters with John Lambert and Billy Libartore, as well as my nightly escapades with Stuart.

But Ambrose's charge that a woman fitting Kimberly's description was seen in Kensington purchasing drugs is among the most ludicrous of his claims. Chronic drug addiction goes against the mechanics of a disciplined life, and Kimberly Ernest's life was disciplined.

Ambrose's depiction of Ernest trekking into Kensington on a regular basis conjures the life of a committed addict. Addicts do not jog on a daily basis and they are not good at keeping a daily routine except when it comes to purchasing or selling drugs. When Ambrose's charges were published, Kimberly's family and friends denied that she ever used drugs. Dorothe Ernest, Kimberly's mother, stated, "It hurts me inside when someone says that about her. I know that's not true. It makes me want to cry. They beat her to death. What more do they want?"

8

RICHARD BRYAN WISE: DANGEROUS GLASSY EYES

Richard Wise—May 19, 1976 to September 6, 2016—died in prison. He was forty years old and still a relatively young man. His incarceration was the result of charges unrelated to the Ernest murder.

I had heard of his death quite by accident from a homeless panhandler in my neighborhood, an older man named Dave I had occasionally had conversations with. Dave would pass through the neighborhood with his book bag, sign, and short beard. His overall look was that of someone who had been beaten down by life and was now the most humble of human beings. In some ways he reminded me of a character out of a Dostoevsky novel, a "Fool for Christ"-type who would babble one moment and then suddenly say something profound. He stood out among the younger homeless who were often aggressive and brash in their mannerisms.

At some point I had mentioned to Dave that I once lived across the street from where the Center City jogger murder occurred. He remembered what I told him about the murder, and that I had once had an encounter with Richie Wise. One day, Dave told me that Richie Wise had died. He said he had heard this through a friend of his who was confined to the same prison as Wise. He also told me that he learned through this prison source that while he was in prison, Richie Wise had a male lover.

While this information could be hearsay, coming from him it struck me as truthful. I had read enough about men in prison to know what can and often happens to the most heterosexually inclined if their confinement lasts long enough. In many ways, Wise fit the stereotype of a violently homophobic young man who is homophobic because he hates the urges he feels within himself. In lashing out at those who display these feelings freely and openly, he is really attacking his own forbidden desires. When my homeless friend spoke about Wise, he did so in the calmest manner: "He died in prison, and when he died he had a partner."

Richard Wise's obituary mentioned nothing of his involvement in the Kimberly Ernest case, neither did it mention his attack on Christopher Cook with a tuna can or his many criminal endeavors when he was a younger, perhaps more careless man. His obituary presented him as a role model, a nearly perfect citizen and father:

Richard Bryan Wise, 40, of Mays Landing, passed from life to life eternal on September 6, 2016. Richard was born and raised in Philadelphia, Pa. He was employed by Lyons Security and worked at the Atlantic City Race Course. Richard was a wonderful man with a great heart. He loved spending time with family and friends. His Goddaughter Abbey was his little princess.

He is predeceased by the loves of his life, daughter, Alyssa and her Mom, Kelly Juhas; his father Leonard; and his brother, Christopher.

He is survived by his mother, Theresa (Josh) of Streetwater; his brother, Eric (Antonia) and their daughters, Abigail and Kaelen, all of Mays Landing. Grandmother Eva E. Harbison of Sweetwater; and his nephew, Ian. He also leaves behind many Aunts, Uncles, cousins and friends who loved him very much.

A Celebration of Life will be held on Thursday, September 15, 2016 at Wimberg Funeral Home, 400 Liverpool Avenue, Egg Harbor City, NJ. Visitation will be from 11:00 am until noon with a service immediately following. Intermment at Egg Harbor City Cemetery. In lieu of flowers, A Go Fund Me Page has been set up to help the family with funeral expenses.

TELEPHONE BOOKS, STRIPPING NUDE, AND ALL MANNER OF ABUSE

In a lawsuit filed by Samuel A. Malat, esquire, of Haddon Heights, New Jersey, on behalf of Richard B. Wise, Alysa Wise, Leonard J. Wise, Theresa A. Wise, and Theresa M. Delillo on April 16, 1997, suing Detectives Tom Augustine, Paul Musi, District Attorney Lynn Abraham, Assistant District Attorney Judith Rubino, the City of Philadelphia, and the Philadelphia Police Police Department (among others), the sum of $75,000,000 and a jury trial was sought by plaintiffs for the violation of their civil rights.

The suit's statement of facts claims that two city detectives (not Augustine or Musi) entered the home of Theresa M. Delillo and seized Plaintiff Richard B. Wise in the presence of Plaintiffs Leonard Wise and Theresa Delillo without permission and without a valid warrant.

According to the suit, the detectives lied when they said they were entering the home because of an outstanding bench warrant for Richard Wise, and then ignored proof produced by Leonard Wise that the bench warrant being referred to had been satisfied.

Two police officers then escorted Richard Wise to the police station. The suit further contends that when the plaintiff arrived at the station, he was subject to "constant and unrelenting physical, mental and emotional abuse during approximately five and one half hours of interrogation by Defendant Detectives Thomas Augustine, Paul Musi and Anthony Tomaino."

At the beginning of the interrogation, detectives forced Plaintiff Richard Wise to strip naked, and then at various times during the "brutal interrogation," Augustine and Musi "repeatedly spit in Richard B. Wise's face." They also repeatedly pulled him around the room by his hair. They then forced Wise to look at "graphic photographs of the body of the deceased Kimberly Ernest."

Augustine and Musi then went further and forced Wise to "stand naked with a forty pound box of computer paper in his outstretched arms."

The detectives would beat Wise whenever he dropped the box of computer paper. When this brand of torture proved insufficient, they then ordered Wise to stand naked "with phone books held up in each hand at shoulder level." The moment that Wise dropped his arms because of the weight, the beatings would be resumed. But even this was tame compared to what came next. Malat claims that Augustine began to choke Wise with an electric cord from an electric typewriter, "forcing it up against his throat."

Apparently Wise had a tattoo on his right forearm of his daughter Alysa's name. The sight of this tattoo, according to Malat, inspired Augustine to repeatedly say, "Do you choke and rape your daughter Alysa?" and "Do you fuck and strangle your daughter Alysa?"

"This caused and continues to cause Plaintiff Richard B. Wise great mental pain and anguish," the document claims.

At this point Detective, Paul Musi ordered the still naked Wise "to turn around and pick up an object from the floor," at which point he kicked Wise in the buttocks, causing him to lose his balance and fall. Laughter accompanied all of these tortures. Detective Anthony Tomaino then got into the act and began placing his forearms to Wise's throat.

The only thing missing from these tortures was St. Sebastian's bow and arrows.

The suit also claimed that during these various tortures, Plaintiff Wise was suffering from sleep deprivation, inferring that he was not in his right mind and making it easy to trick him into signing "a false and concocted statement."

"The detectives wore Plaintiff Richard B. Wise down, and his will was overborn, so that he agreed to give a statement."

The torture was supposed to have lasted over a period of five and a half hours.

At that point, according to Ambrose, Detective William Egenlauf had a false and concocted statement typed up for Wise's signature. Egenlauf allowed Wise to read the first two pages of the typed statement before signing them, leading Wise to assume (according to Ambrose) that he was signing a statement filled with background information he had given as to his relationship to Herbert Haak. The remaining pages of the statement that Egenlauf made Wise sign without reading them contained statements that Wise never made.

The false statements that Wise was forced to sign were statements made by the convicted felon John Hall, "who was trying to improve his own situation in prison."

Ambrose wrote that the trickery employed by Egenlauf to get Wise to sign without reading the pages of the statement "containing a false and concocted story" was conducted without the benefit of a video tape of the process. Ambrose charges the City of Philadelphia, the Philadelphia Police Department, and the defendant detectives named in his document with willful ignorance and a total disregard of Wise's constitutional rights because they failed to corroborate and verify the authenticity of the alleged statements of a suspect. The document accuses Philadelphia of being behind the times for its refusal to install such video equipment and procedures which by 1995 had become standard practice in other large metropolitan cities.

Ambrose stated that the action of the defendants would force Wise's daughter Alysa "to grow up with the social stigma wrongfully imposed upon the family by this destruction of Richard W. Wise's reputation in the community."

This false testimony cased Wise to suffer repeated death threats from other inmates while he was in jail awaiting trial for the murder of Kimberly Ernest, "causing him great emotional distress and fear for his life and physical safety."

Ambrose charged that the inculpatory evidence pointing to other suspects was ignored by Defendant District Attorney Lynn Abraham and Defendant Assistant Attorney Judi Rubino, including the discovery of a jewelry receipt at the crime scene which had the employment address and employee number of alternative suspect Mr. J. L. on it.

Other inculpatory evidence cited by Ambrose includes that face that Lambert was seen (by Libartore) outside smoking crack in the area of the murder scene and at the time of the murder.

The most egregious charge, however, is Ambrose's mostly true observation that it was the policy and the practice of the City of Philadelphia and the Philadelphia Police to cover up the actions of certain police officers and detectives who used excessive force and physical and verbal abuse of suspects.

This was a convenient statement of fact thrown over the Haak-Wise case like a winter quilt as if it was just another typical case of police abuse.

The plaintiffs in Ambrose's suit demanded the sum of $75,000,000.00 in exemplary damages. Leonard J. Wise, Richie Wise's father, signed the court document on April 16, 1997.

(MORE) HERBERT HAAK

Ambrose's Civil Action No. 97-6634 filed on October 23, 1997 in the U.S. District Court for the Eastern District of Pennsylvania on behalf of Herbert C. P. Haak for a sum to be fixed by the jury, plus punitive damages, interest, costs, and attorney's fees, had a long list of defendants, including the City of Philadelphia, Police Commissioner Richard Neal, John Hall, John Murphy, warden of the Philadelphia Prison system, detectives Thomas Augustine, Paul Musi, Eugene Wyatt, Charles Boyle, Dennis Dusak, and various minor prison officials.

The suit claimed that on or about November 18, 1995, defendants Boyle and Wyatt seized Haak from a Bucks County correctional facility where he had been residing because of a probation violation, and transported him to the Philadelphia Homicide Division in connection with the murder of Kimberly Ernest.

The suit contends that Haak was subject to unrelenting physical, mental, and emotional torture during a six-hour illegal interrogation. The colorful document states that Haak was forced to strip naked after which he was battered about his head, chest, and stomach. The detectives then spit in Haak's face while "defendant Augustine choked plaintiff to the point where he could not breathe."

There were also a series of pummels to the plaintiff's head, face, chest, and stomach and additional bouts of verbal and emotional abuse. Augustine, it was claimed, rubbed his feet on the plaintiff's face and chest and then pulled him by the hair to force him to look at graphic photographs of Kimberly Ernest's body (the same photos that I saw in Ambrose's office). While all this was going on, Haak made one request to see a lawyer but was told by detective Wyatt that "he watched too much television."

The suit claimed that Augustine then forced Haak to sign blank police confession forms.

The document claims that the detectives took the course of action they did because they believed the story told to them by John Hall, Haak's stepfather, who had "falsely informed police that he had been told by plaintiff that plaintiff had committed the Ernest murder."

John Hall is described as a professional informant who made up the alleged story about Haak's alleged confession in retaliation for Haak's 1994 report to police that Hall had left his stepdaughter, age twelve, at home, without parental care or supervision , for four months for which Hall was arrested, convicted, and jailed.

On November 30, 1995, Haak was arrested and charged with murdering, raping, kidnapping, and unlawfully restraining Kimberly Ernest. While awaiting trial, he was moved from Curran Fromhold Correctional Facility to the Philadelphia Industrial Correctional Center, where he was later assaulted and beaten up (Haak's nose was broken) by inmates. Ambrose claims that Haak's wounds went unattended for two days. Prison officials waited three months before they allowed Haak to seek medical attention to have his nose reset, but the waiting period proved too long a time and he would have to consult a plastic surgeon for surgery. Prison officials, however, caused further delays despite letters from Haak's lawyer and Haak's repeated sick call requests. Surgery was finally scheduled for March 1997 but without warning Prison Health Services, Inc. cancelled Haak's surgery.

When a jury acquitted Haak of all charges related to the murder of Kimberly Ernest on March 14, 1997, Haak was not freed but remained in prison as a result of another incident which had occurred in October 1996, an incident that Ambrose claims was "perpetuated by Augustine and Dusak." That incident has all the *noir* elements of a television police drama.

Haak claims that he was taken by two officers to a forest outside the detention center where his handcuffs were removed and where he was told by the two officers who had their guns drawn, to run. Haak says that he refused to run.

On the same day, the same two officers took Haak to the Police Administration building and delivered him into the hands of Dusak and Augustine where he was charged with two counts of carjacking and robbery (fabricated, according to Ambrose.) Augustine and Dusak then proceeded to beat Haak up. In May 1997, Haak underwent surgery to have his nose fixed. The surgery also alleviated Haak's chronic headaches and pain as a result of the initial injury one year before.

Haak's rabbit hole of misfortunes was not about to end, however, because the delivery of the nasal spray proscribed by surgeons following the surgery to aid in his recovery was significantly delayed.

The scenario worsened when, two days following nose surgery, Haak visited an oral surgeon for dental care and the surgeon, like a character out of a Stephen

King novel, "pushed his hands on the plaintiff's bandaged nose for the purpose of performing a dental procedure and immediately re-broke it." Haak then had to undergo a second surgery in which his nose had to be re-broken and reset.

When the charges of robbery and carjacking that Ambrose claims were fabricated by Augustine and Dusak were squashed by the court, Haak was released from prison on July 3, 1997.

9

THE FATHER

Jay Lambert, father of John Lambert, lives with his wife, Barbara, in a retirement community in Connecticut.

"We are outside Newport," he said, "we're actually the last piece of property between Middletown and Newport. It takes us 5 to 7 miles to get into Newport. Every once in a while I will say to my wife, Barbara, 'Oh, let's go on the Mile Drive,' where it's one mansion after another."

I was able to contact Jay Lambert when Tom Augustine called me and announced that he was able to obtain Jay Lambert's phone number. When I called Jay Lambert, I asked him if I could talk to him about his son, the accusations leveled against him, and about the case in general.

I had not heard Jay Lambert's voice since our legal dealings in the mid-1990s when I testified on his behalf during his lawsuit against Malat and Ambrose who had defamed his son in their lawsuit against a wide range of individuals like Tom Augustine, Dusak, the City of Philadelphia, and the Philadelphia Police Department.

Lambert told me that he had retired almost twenty years ago and that he does not miss Philadelphia. "The only thing I miss is my daughter who is up in New Hope, Pennsylvania and who is doing well," he said. I brought up the Kimberly Ernest murder and mentioned the names Herbert Haak and Richie Wise. "I really know nothing about the murder or the circumstances. I really don't, and I never tried to find out. I assumed that Beau [John Lambert] had nothing whatsoever to do with it. That's what he insisted."

Lambert said that Beau told him that he was being targeted by Fred Ambrose for the murder:

Beau told me, "Gee, I saw that girl [Kimberly Ernest] in a couple of bars down in Center City, and that was it." I'm not sure that he spoke to her but I think he would have said hello to her at least. My son lived in Center City and he bumped into that girl a couple of times. They knew each other but I never found out from Beau what the status of the friendship was. She used to frequent bars. Beau would see her every once in a while in a bar and talk to her and that was about it. But, we never did find out why they targeted him. We never found that out other than the supposition that he knew her. As for the facts surrounding the case, I never understood what they were. It was pathetic finger pointing. I think it was two strangers who picked Kimberly Ernest up in a bar—"Okay, we'll drive you home"—and that was the end of her.

As dumb as these people are—Haak and Wise—certainly they never had anything to do with the murder itself…. You know what? I didn't even know that they had confessed to the case.

I was surprised when Lambert said, "I'm just warning you. You have absolutely no idea what happened. I would imagine just about anybody driving by could have done it. It could have been somebody she knew, it could have been somebody she didn't know. I really have absolutely no idea at all. I knew that it was out of character for Beau to do anything like that. He never got caught in being part of any kind of violent crime. He did do drugs. That was his whole life. Fred Ambrose charging Beau with the crime was the sheerest nonsense."

Lambert mentioned Samuel Malat and Fred Ambrose. "They were the prime defendants. Ambrose was the ringleader and the ringleader was missing," he said.

Lambert was referring to Ambrose's disappearance when the trial got underway for Lambert's countersuit of $40 million:

We had absolutely no idea where Ambrose was at the time of the trial, which was perfectly fine with me. You know, we could have said anything during the trial of that case and it would have made perfect sense to the judge. Their three   attorneys were not objecting. Ambrose escaped to England and Europe then he tried to gain admission to the Bar in the state of California. And was immediately arrested by federal agents and shipped back to Philadelphia. Yes, he was in England, as I recall. He was actually arrested in a courtroom in southern California where they were going to admit him.

Ambrose, Lambert says, was "laid back but incompetent," while Samuel Malat, who could only practice in New Jersey, struck Lambert as impossibly stupid. "I have absolutely no idea at all how anybody that stupid could be a lawyer," he said:

> During the trial, he didn't even realize that you could object. He couldn't defend himself let alone anybody else.
>
> Because Fred Ambrose had disappeared at the time of the trial, he did not have representation and had a judgment entered against him.
>
> The Fred Ambrose team of lawyers who were there were probably the worst lawyers I have ever run across. Malat really stuck out because he was just so absolutely incompetent. He was just lost in the courtroom. I don't know how a lawyer like that ever got a law degree. The judge despised Fred Ambrose. I think this was the easiest trial I ever had.

Lambert says that he tried to find out how Kimberly Ernest was killed, but that that process was like falling down a rat hole.

"Once you got into it, that's it, there's no place to go." About Haak and Wise's trial or the actual crime, he says he knows nothing about it. "What could I contribute other than to say that I was in a bogus law suit by a couple of attorneys that were claiming that we had some sort of involvement?"

Beau, Lambert said, seemed like an easy scapegoat. "As it turned out, simply because of the incompetency of counsel, they [Ambrose and Malat] got whacked with a 40 million judgment. I never understood how any of those people were practicing law. We just did enough work to present a case. God was on our side."

During our conversation, Lambert kept coming back to his son. "It really might be interesting to find out why Fred Ambrose targeted Beau. Coming up with a reason would be pure speculation on my part other than Beau knew her from barrooms. I can remember asking him how many times did you see her and he said, 'Oh maybe 3 or 4 times and we just said hi.'"

FUGITIVE JUSTICE

The Pennsylvania Department of Transportation driver demographics on Fred John Ambrose, Jr. reads like this: Born on June 1, 1952; blue eyes, 72 inches tall; places of residence as of April 4, 2000, Frazer/Malvern, Pennsylvania. Corrective lenses; organ donor.

On December 15, 2004, *The Philadelphia Inquirer* published the following headline:

"Bala Cynwyd Lawyer is arrested in California":

A Bala Cynwyd lawyer who vanished three years ago amid allegations that he was stealing from clients has been arrested in California on federal fraud charges.

Fred John Ambrose Jr., 52, was charged Monday with bank fraud and mail fraud and accused of bilking clients out of insurance settlements, totaling $160,950. He was arrested after federal authorities in Philadelphia tracked him to Culver City, California, where he had been living.

Authorities said Ambrose, a personal injury lawyer, negotiated settlements for clients without telling them, then forged their signatures, cashed the checks, and pocketed the money.

Ambrose, formerly of West Chester, fled Pennsylvania in 2001, leaving behind a wife and two children and abandoning his law practice. He left after some clients accused him of defrauding them. The clients contacted the state Office of Disciplinary Counsel, which handles complaints against lawyers.

That office notified federal authorities, who began an investigation that eventually led a grand jury to indict Ambrose on fraud charges. The indictment remained sealed while Ambrose's whereabouts were unknown.

Ambrose's license to practice law in Pennsylvania was suspended in June 2001. His license to practice law in California was suspended the following year after the bar association learned of the Pennsylvania sanction.

Initially, Ambrose did not fight the California suspension, but this week, he appealed to the state bar court—and that put investigators on his trail.

On Monday, as Ambrose appeared at the courthouse for a hearing on the license suspension, federal authorities placed him under arrest.

Ambrose, who was released on bond, could not be reached for comment.

Efforts to reach Ambrose's wife, Mary, were unsuccessful.

Before he left the area [Philadelphia], Ambrose was entangled in a law suit arising from the Center City jogger case. He represented a man accused of rape in the jogger case and in the course of defending him suggested that another man had committed the crime.

The other man, John Lambert, sued Ambrose. Lambert and his family later won a 40.8 million defamation settlement against Ambrose and his law partners. A lawyer for the Lambert family declined to comment yesterday.

John Lambert died of a drug overdose at age twenty-seven on February 1, 1999. "Lambert met his fate in Room 50 of the Hallmark Hotel on Rte. 130 in lovely Cinnaminson, N.J.," wrote Howard Altman in a *City Paper* piece, "The Never Ending

Story," in February 1999. "Recently released from prison, where he was serving time for a parole violation, Lambert was staying at the Hallmark with his lover. At 12:42 a.m. on Monday Feb. 1, rescue squads received a call to rush to the hotel. Lambert was removed from the hotel room—still breathing—and taken to Kennedy Memorial Hospital in Cherry Hill, where he died later that day."

Lambert filed the original defamation lawsuit before his death. In August 2002, Jay and Barbara Lambert won a $40.8 million defamation verdict in Common Pleas Court.

Fred Ambrose and Samuel Malat were held liable, as were investigators Stephen Stouffer and Albert Tyree (Skip Thomas) and Leonard Wise. Common Pleas Court Judge Alan Tereshko, who presided at the trial, barred the defendants from putting on a defense.

As *The Philadelphia Inquirer* reported in 2002, "The jury rendered its $40.8 million verdict, which included $21 million in punitive damages against Ambrose and $11 million against Malat. Other defendants were ordered to pay a total of $275,000 in punitive damages. The $8.5 million compensatory award was leveled against all five defendants."

The Inquirer quoted Ambrose's claim that there was a conspiracy to protect John Lambert because Jay Lambert was a partner in the prominent law firm of Duane Morris.

Howard Altman wrote in *Philadelphia City Paper* that the verdict was delivered "in the ornate, columned chambers of Courtroom 243 in City Hall—made famous by the movies *Philadelphia* and *Witness*."

Altman quoted a juror after the verdict was announced: "We felt that people can't just go around saying what they want about other people without having consequences for their actions and words. You can't say things about other people without having evidence, and in this case there was no evidence to back up what they were saying."

In yet another trial—this one a check fraud trial involving Herbert Haak in which Haak passed a worthless $6,465 check in 1999 while buying computer equipment—the *Philadelphia Daily News* reported that Haak purchased four personal computers and a laptop and paid with a phony check. The check was out of a non-existing account.

The courtroom was empty, although there was one observer present, Tom Augustine, "sitting in the third row ... awaiting a call to testify at a murder trial in a nearby room." When Haak noticed Augustine in the courtroom, defense attorney Fred Ambrose attempted to win an acquittal despite the fact that the U.S. Justice Department found no evidence that Wise or Haak had been abused during their questioning by Augustine and Sgt. Paul Musi. The judge, Gary S. Glazer, shut down Ambrose's plea for an acquittal.

In June 2001, Howard Altman wrote a piece for *Philadelphia City Paper* entitled "Judi's Justice."

Assistant District Attorney Judi Frankel Rubino, as the chief prosecutor in the Haak-Wise case, was also the longest serving ADA in Lynne Abraham's office. Rubino went into the Haak–Wise trial with a perfect record: she had never lost a major case until the Center City jogger case.

Rubino, who rarely gave interviews, shared with Altman the distress she felt when Fred Ambrose obtained copies of her credit report.

"Ambrose's motives for going after these credit histories is unclear, and he is not around to answer questions. His wife, Mary, filed a Missing Persons Report on him in April, and repeated efforts to discover his whereabouts have proven unsuccessful. It seems likely, however, that he was trying to find ways to discredit anyone remotely connected with the alleged 'conspiracy,'" Altman wrote.

According to Altman, Ambrose was also able to obtain a report on Jay Jewell Lambert, "a patrician partner at Duane Morris & Heckscher whose son John would be named by Ambrose as 'the real killer' of Ernest."

He also went after Homicide Detective Thomas Augustine's and Dennis Dusak's credit report.

"The Lambert thing was really unbelievable," Rubino told Altman. "I really think that they killed [John] Lambert. I mean, I think that he died as a result of all this stuff."

The interview continues:

"The problem wasn't with the DNA, it was with the medical examiner," says Rubino bluntly. "He wrote his report wrong. This is a situation where there were fresh vaginal tears and no sperm, but no rectal tears, with a small quantity of whole, degenerated sperm, and in his report the medical examiner said that the rectal area, quote, 'was further evidence of sexual assault.' This is incorrect; it was not."

Then there were the confessions that weren't. Rubino argued in court that, despite claims by Haak and Wise of being beaten into signing confessions, nothing of the kind ever happened. She cited microscopic evidence that contradicted the claim of Haak and Wise that they had signed blank pages.

There were also witnesses who couldn't be used, like Haak's father-in-law, who tried to be helpful by making up fake evidence. By introducing Haak's parents, Rubino had hoped to show that Wise not only killed Kimberly Ernest, but threatened the life of Haak's mother Phyllis Hall as well.

"I was just afraid to put her on," Rubino says, resigned to being stuck with bad evidence. "I am not going to put on any witness that's lying. Plus, Ritchie [Wise] went to her house, and threatened her: 'If you tell the police what I did with your son, we'll kill him and your boyfriend too.'"

Rubino told Altman that she believed that the deck was stacked against her as far as the jury went.

It was around the time of the O.J. Simpson trial, and the buffoonery of the L.A. prosecutor's office was not playing well in this Philadelphia courtroom.

"We know that the foreman said to the other jurors, 'Well, it took the O.J. jury 20 minutes, let's see if we can beat it.'"

There were other problems with the jury, she says.

"We found out later that one of the jurors had a cell phone with him in the hotel, and even though they were sequestered, he was talking to people," Rubino says.

Courthouse sources, she adds, reported to her that jurors "bought a T-shirt for the court officer. It was a Mickey Mouse T-shirt, and supposedly for a 'Mickey Mouse' case. She [the court officer] didn't tell the judge. So apparently [the jury and the officer] had talked about [the case] beforehand. I mean, everything was stacked against us."

There is even testimony, in the form of a statement taken by a private investigator working for the city, that a juror was bribed.

"You asked me if I was positive that a juror was paid off, and I told you I was positive," said a convicted con man named John Groff, who claimed the bribery was at the behest of Sam Malat, the lawyer who represented Wise in the civil suit against the city, and who now, in Ambrose's absence, has taken over all his cases.

Malat vociferously denies that, saying "there is not one ounce of truth in the statement" made by Groff, who had been his office assistant. "I have a restraining order against him because he threatened the life of a family member."

Efforts to reach Groff, including letters to the prison in New Jersey where he was once incarcerated, have been unsuccessful.

"It does not surprise me at all," says Rubino about the possibility that a juror was bribed. "Given everything those guys have done ever since [the trial]."

Add it all up, Rubino says, and you have a mess. The jury came back in less than three hours and Haak and Wise walked.

"Oh, it was just horrible," says Rubino, over the din of noon diners. "Because we knew that they were guilty. I still have no doubt that they were guilty. And it was one of the very few cases over 30 years of prosecuting that came out bad, and I think that they beat a case on which they should have been convicted. And if they had a juror bribed, then that's even more evidence of it."

10

THE MOTHER

We all survive more than we think we can.

Joan Didion

Dorothe Ernest says that when her daughter, Kimberly, lived in Perth, Australia, she was often mistaken for actress Nicole Kidman:

> Her natural hair color is red and it is very curly, and Kim said it was a real hoot to get mistaken for Nicole Kidman because for a while she could really carry it off. When Nicole Kidman was first in movies she had hair exactly like Kim's. A huge head of red, curly, curly curls. She was full of life.
>
> Kim got such a kick out of people coming up to her and looking at her and asking if she was Nicole Kidman. You know, as a child she put her various hats on the wall like they were paintings. In high school she went to Iceland to plant trees, then in her junior year she didn't want to do what everyone else did when they went to Australia—they went to Sydney—but she went to Perth where she enjoyed playing with kangaroos.

There was so much to ask Dorothe Ernest, so much that I was curious about. The idea to try and contact her came shortly after my talks with Tom Augustine. I did a Google search never expecting to find her address, but there it was. Or was it? I wrote Dorothe Ernest, told her about the project I was working on, and included a business card in the mix. I waited a couple of weeks and when I did not receive a reply, I decided to call her. Dorothe answered the phone and graciously told me that she had received my letter and was just taking some time to get back to me. She also said that she had to think about answering me because she did not know what kind of book I was writing, or how I would portray her daughter.

"When I first got your note," Dorothe told me, "I told myself 'I'll even spend the money to go to Philadelphia to meet you.' I want the book done right."

After these introductory remarks, Dorothe began to feel comfortable talking to me and she started to talk about the murder. I had not expected her to reveal so much during that first phone call, especially when my intention was to set up a time for a phone interview once we agreed to one.

"This is not a cold case because they know who killed her. It's not set up someplace as a cold case—they are not going to spend time and energy looking for someone when they know who did it. Those two [Haak and Wise] cannot be tried again," she said.

Dorothe told me that she thought about filing a civil case when Haak and Wise were acquitted but then decided, "What is this for? It's not going to bring Kimberly back. But I wanted some kind of justice. If your book makes people care about her then that's all I'm asking. Do you know what I'm saying?"

The subject of DNA came up:

Nowadays we are so good with DNA. Her shoes and her socks were on and her jogging bra was on pulled up over her breast. She had that on. They said there was not one speck of DNA. I don't believe it. Somebody told me—I don't know if it was a detective or somebody—that the particular man who did the autopsy was not good. In the past this man had claimed that a victim was a female when it was really a male, or a male when it was really a female, but he didn't get the sex right. They also had Kimberly as 2 inches taller—she was 5' 8", they had her as 5' 10"—and my comment about that is, "Dead bodies don't wiggle."

How could they be off on her height? Two inches off on her height is a fairly large amount. If they took any care, how could they be off on her height?

Dorothe told me that she was contacted by a gentleman from Northwestern University, a lawyer:

He's from a center/clinic where they try to get people out of jail who have been found guilty when they didn't do the crime. I've talked to him on numerous occasions for about a year. I told him that they still have Kimberly's sneakers and socks and her jogging bra. I think if these items have been kept in any kind of relatively clean environment then they could re-examine these items. That's what the lawyer was wanting to do, and he asked me to talk about it because there's now a new person who has something to do with the DNA and he was going to try and get them to open up that box of Kim's items. I think this could happen, and to me your book might raise the pressure for them to do that. I would love for them to do that. That's really one of the reasons I'm talking to you. The DNA they are able to find is unbelievable, and the fact that they found nothing back then!

Dorothe trailed off as if reliving a painful memory. I asked her why her daughter moved to Philadelphia. "My fault," she answered abruptly:

I always thought Philadelphia was a very exciting town because of its history. Also, Kim didn't have a car—she actually never asked me for a car—but I've lived in Philadelphia for 2 months with my husband when I was first married. Philadelphia is a very walkable city, and I suggested Philadelphia.... Not that she always took my advice but it was my suggestion. Then she was thinking about going to law school but a couple of her friends were in law school and they hated it. So I said, "Why don't you be a paralegal, work in the field, and see if you like it and then you can tolerate going through a couple years of miserable law school—if that's how bad it is."

There was another pause in the conversation, no doubt caused by a flood of memories. "I've lived in this house for 41 years. I'm not a transient kind of person.... Of course, they reason I've been stammering and sometimes having a hard time finding words is that this is very emotional."

I was not getting the sense that Dorothe was stammering but perhaps in her mind she was not sounding as she thought she should have sounded. "A mother would do almost anything for her child," she continued:

I won't say "almost"; a mother would do anything—no, let me change it, I would do anything to help Kim. On her birthday I go to the bakery and get a big brown cake, a big round loaf of bread uncut and I spread peanut butter all over the sides and top and sprinkled it with bird seed, and put a candle in the middle and take it up to her grave so we can have a birthday party with the deer, birds and squirrels. They eat the cake. That brown loaf of bread always disappears relatively fast. It's in a very old cemetery where my parents and grandparents are...

Dorothe told me that Kimberly's younger sister, "is still actively grieving her sister's death—ah yes, the two were inseparable."

With that, she goes into the sisters' histories. "I got a call from the telephone company once," she tells me, "announcing that I obviously had a problem because on my bill were calls from Australia and Venezuela, but both my daughters were in different countries at one point. The phone company asked if they could help me with this but I told them that I always pay the phone bill and they were not to worry. I said, 'I always pay the phone bill. My girls are allowed to buy any book—I will pay for any book if they read it and they can talk to each other as many times as they want and as long as they want.'"

Then, Dorothe told me something extraordinary. She said that somebody from Kimberly's professional world attended her funeral in Illinois; a man that she suspected had been intimate with her daughter because he made the time to fly out from Philadelphia to be there.

After the funeral, Dorothe and the man went out to dinner. The man ordered a glass of wine with his food and at some point during the meal excused himself to go to the bathroom. When he was gone, Dorothe says she reached for the man's white wine glass and held it as the man returned to the table. When the man was seated, she indicated the glass and said, "I have your wine glass. I have your DNA. I want you to tell me if you were with Kim the night before her death. I want to know if you were her last lover."

The implication here is profound.

The semen found in Kimberly's body did not match either Haak's or Wise's DNA, a discovery that led to their acquittal. During the search among Kimberly's boyfriends who volunteered to come forward for a DNA test, there was the accountant—my friend Chuck—who was brave enough to be tested and even to be filmed by TV cameras despite his being a married man. It was Augustine who told me that the accountant consented on the spot if it would help convict the killers.

The man from Kimberly's professional orbit, however, did not come forward, but now here he was sitting in front of Dorothe Ernest who held his glass of wine with his DNA, asking forcibly but politely if he was the missing DNA link.

Although Dorothe was vague on what the man said to her as she held his wine glass, the implication was clear: He had been with Kimberly the night before her death. But there was a problem. He was married with children. What would such a revelation do to his marriage?

Dorothe said there was not much she could do with the information because it made no sense to her to ruin somebody's life:

Part of me is angry because if this man had had the courage and the guts to say, "Look, here's my DNA and that's what you found," it would have been a very different outcome.

I'm a psychotherapist so the last thing I want to do is hurt someone … anyway,
I struggle with that. But I think if that could have been made public, and if the
jury had had a chance to see how badly she was beaten …

Dorothe let the sentence drop and in a few seconds recovered and reflected on the
trial and the acquittal: "The judge told me that you never know what a jury's going
to do. When I heard that I made the decision if I were ever in a situation where
I could choose between a jury and a decision by a judge, I would pick a judge."

SOMETHING TERRIBLE HAS HAPPENED IN PHILADELPHIA

Dorothe Ernest did not find out that her daughter Kimberly died until 1 p.m. on
November 2, 1995. "It was a Thursday morning around Noon when I got a call from my
former husband's administrative assistant saying that she and Terry wanted to come
see me that afternoon," she says. "I'm a psychotherapist and I had patients scheduled
for that afternoon. I said no, then I asked, 'What is this about? Is Terry [her former
husband] in surgery? Is he in clinic? Is he in his research lab? Put him on the phone.'"

The assistant said that she could not put Terry on the phone.

"Then I can't invite you to come this afternoon because I'm not going to cancel
patients if this is not important," Dorothe told her.

The assistant answered that the only thing she could say was that "something
terrible has happened in Philadelphia."

Dorothe then called Kimberly's apartment and was greeted with her daughter's
cheery message, "Hi, this is Kim…"

"Of course she's not home in her apartment, it's a work day," Dorothe reminded
herself. She then called Kimberly's work number and says she was greeted with
the following recorded message: "Due to an emergency, the offices are closed,
but if you have to get a hold of someone, call this number…"

She recalled that there had something in the news about a series of bombings
in Philadelphia, and she wondered if maybe there had been a bomb that went
off on Kimberly's street or in her building.

She called the number given out by Kim's law firm. "This is Dorothe Ernest,
I'm Kimberly Ernest's mother. I believe I need to talk to someone. May I speak
with her boss?"

When her daughter's boss, Russell Cunningham, got on the line, he said, "I
thought the police or your husband would have notified you…. Kimberly has
been found dead…"

"I feel very bad. The guy never thought he'd have to tell me," Dorothe confesses and says the news was like "a blast white out time."

"Well, why didn't you bother to call me," she said to Cunningham.

Dorothe says she was cross, but when she calmed down, she asked Cunningham to give her a direct number to the police rather than a general number.

She says that "everything kind of clicked together" when Cunningham told her "she's dead." She immediately understood why Terry, her ex-husband, could not talk and why his assistant was trying to protect him.

When she called the detective and got the information, she once again had to ask, "Why didn't you call me? Just because I'm divorced I am still her mother." The detective apologized and explained that they had notified her father and assumed that he had told her, "which he had not," Dorothy adds.

Dorothe looked at the clock and saw that it was five minutes to 1 p.m. A panic set in as she sat down to collect herself.

She says she tried calling her client to tell her not to come, but there was no answer. At that moment, she looked out the window and to the right of her vision she saw the client pulling up in her car. She saw the TV camera truck coming up the small hill where her house was located. The first thing she had to do was to tell her client to go home.

"I ran outside and said to her, 'Listen very carefully, please. There's been a terrible emergency. I can't see you today. Please go right away because I can see the police and the camera truck coming up the hill.' I'm protective of clients and I didn't want her to be traumatized. The whole thing was horror on top of horror."

Following the news truck, her husband Terry and his assistant arrived by car. Dorothe says she did the TV interview while a gaggle of people surrounded her house. She says that she felt like a series of red "alert" sound alarms were going off in her head.

Dorothe came to Philadelphia the following day. "The city was wonderful to me," she recalled:

I stayed in a nice small hotel. The people of Philadelphia, the police, the mayor—I was shocked at their hospitality. I would go into a restaurant to eat dinner and all of a sudden the waiters would say, "The couple at such-and-such a table have paid for your dinner." I was so easily recognizable because it was so fresh in the news. I even commented to the police, "Why are you being so nice to me? You guys are rough policeman." These are detectives, not the school crossing guards. Everyone seemed to take her death into their own life....

You know, this was the beautiful girl next door and how could this have happened?

Dorothe said that she wanted to visit the stairwell at 21st and Pine Streets but was told, "No, no, you can't do that."

She said she does not recall when she visited it, that it could have been on a subsequent trip to the city, but she knew she had to go there despite the objections, just as she realized that she had to go to the morgue to identify Kim. Initially, the morgue showed her images of Kim on a TV screen. "I'm sorry," Dorothe said. "I can't recognize her. I want to see her." She was told, "No, you can't do that."

"Then I said, 'Well, I don't recognize her.' I have a lot of tenacity when I need to. The screen was black and white; it wasn't very distinct and her face was very, very distorted and swollen from the blows. Finally they said, 'Okay,' so I took the elevator down—my younger daughter has never forgiven me for this—and said, 'I'm going down to see her. You can come down to see her.' My daughter followed me into the elevator. Anyway, my daughter wished that she had never seen her because it was so horrifying."

Dorothe describes what happened once she got off the elevator. "I saw them wheeling a gurney up a long skinny hallway. She was covered up with a sheet, tags on her toe, and they lifted back the sheet so I could see her face and in her curly hair I pulled out leaves and little sticks—what mothers do is get the hair out of your kid's eyes. It's an instinctual thing, where you touch your child's forehead and push the bangs away. I picked out leaves and little twigs and then I wanted to pull the sheet down in my sense of disbelief but the attendant didn't want me to pull the sheet down. He didn't want me to see the autopsy scar. I did not pull the sheet down, I'd been bossy enough," Dorothe added with a small therapeutic laugh.

"At that point I didn't know that the autopsy was a farce. They had her down as being 2 inches taller than she really was. Dead bodies don't wiggle. If they couldn't even get her height accurate, what else did they miss? All I knew at the time was that I was comforting my daughter by touching her hair. "

CONFRONTATION WITH JUDI RUBINO

Later, when Dorothe went to ask Judi Rubino for the autopsy report, Rubino told her "No, you can't see that," at which Dorothy replied, "Sorry, I have to see that. I'm her mother and I'm entitled."

"So she handed me the autopsy report and I looked through it and I said, 'Wait a minute, she's not 5' 10" she's 5' 8" or 5' 7½"'" and then Judi Rubino snatched the report out of my hand. I had just seen it for 5 seconds and she said, 'That's why I didn't want you to see the autopsy report!'—meaning, you're just going to start trouble and getting into her business."

"But information allows me to make good decisions. When I don't have information I have nowhere to put my thoughts. I have to have facts," Dorothe told me.

Dorothe admits that she was very aggressive with Rubino. "I really didn't like it when Judi Rubino snatched it out of my hand. Her attitude was she had a job to do and I had no role in that job." Later, Dorothe says she talked about the discrepancy in the autopsy report to the detectives and was told that the man who did the autopsy had a reputation for making mistakes, and that at one point he had misidentified the sex of a body that was decomposed.

Dorothe says she got along famously with the Philadelphia detectives. "The detectives were a good gang of guys. We went to a dinner. It was a party for somebody and they invited me to go along. I saw them as friends not detectives. They were friends helping me. That meant a great deal to me. They were concerned about my well being because I felt very isolated and alone."

She told me that she never bought the John Lambert story. About Ambrose's claim that Lambert and Kimberly were close friends, she said that "Kim knew everybody."

"When Kim first went to Philadelphia before she went to paralegal school, she worked for Honeywell, the heating and cooling place. The guys told me that Kim was the kind of young woman who could talk football and sports with the guys. She was cool..."

"I was in Philadelphia for a couple of days to empty her apartment," Dorothe said. "Kim was a tidy mouse, she was a very organized girl but she wasn't the best housekeeper. I remember on a subsequent visit I demanded to see the stairwell at 21st and Pine. They said no, that would be too hard. But I said, 'Either help me to get to it or I'll do it when you leave. I need to see where she was alive.'"

A dog's bark interrupts our conversation. "I have a dog too!" Dorothe laughs. Part of Dorothe Ernest's strength obviously comes from her sense of humor.

Russ Cunningham, Kim's boss, was saying then that there should be plaque made up, and it should read something like, "This is the spot where the jogger, etc."... The jogger community got behind the idea of a bronze plague but something about it didn't sit well with me. At the marathon race shortly after the murder there were T-shirts that read, "Run Kim Run" and "Go Kim." It warms my heart that the running community got behind her.

Kim was a graduate of Lawrence University in Wisconsin. After she got her BA she moved to Philadelphia and went to the Philadelphia school of paralegals where she got an advanced degree. She was a very independent person, naturally intelligent. She didn't have to work for her grades. She had a lot of ability. After her murder I had a long conversation with Mayor Rendell at her memorial service. The mayor cried.

Arthur Larrabee, one of law partners at Larrabee and Cunningham [the firm now has three names, Cunningham & Larrabee] kept asking me where I wanted to have her McGowan memorial service, and I said, "I don't know. I can't make that decision right now." Then I learned that Arthur was a Quaker and that the Arch Street Meeting House was the first Quaker church in the USA. I thought, "how perfect because I like Quakers, I like the philosophy of Quakers, I like the fact that no one is the boss and everyone is allowed to speak at Quaker meetings." So, Kim had two funerals. At the memorial in Philadelphia after the service there were refreshments and a homeless man came up to me and said, "I want you to know that we cared about her," implying that it's not just the fancy people and the mayor saying nice things.

Everyone went out of their way to be gracious and sensitive, and I kept thinking of the City of Brotherly Love. Philadelphia for me really lived up to that. The people including the rough old policemen were so kind. All during my stay in Philadelphia and at the service my sister was glued to my side. She gave me tremendous support. We have laughed in subsequent years the way that she was identified in newspaper articles: "Dorothe Ernest and her Unknown Escort," because my sister doesn't like a lot of publicity at all.

I asked Dorothe when she first heard that the police were on the trail of the killers. "When I came back to Philadelphia one time to clean out Kim's apartment, I was picked up by police detectives at the airport and they said they had some good leads on the killer but couldn't tell me anything. They assured me that they weren't going to sleep, they were going to figure it out, that they were on the case."

I asked her about the trial and whether or not she looked into the faces of Haak or Wise. "When I first saw photos of Richie Wise and then when I saw the replay on the TV when I was in Philadelphia of his arrest, Richie Wise was a very slight wimpy looking young boy, and his face was all broken out, and when they presented him a year and a couple of months after the murder for the trial, he was dressed in a white shirt and a tie. He looked like a Sunday School teacher. He had 14 months or whatever of food, clothing and shelter and cleaned up pretty nicely."

Seeing this version of Wise made her wish that the court could see him at the time of his arrest. "I really wish the jury could have seen the photo taken in the morgue and taken of Kim's body in the stairwell," she added. "I asked Judi Rubino that question and she said, 'It would be too upsetting for them to see it.' I told Rubino, 'That's ridiculous.'"

Indeed, why was the jury protected from the ugly reality of that crime? Why this attempt by Rubino at self-sabotage? Rubino had never lost a big case in her thirty-some years as ADA, but something inside her seemed to be unraveling in this case.

"I was at odds with Judi Rubino from the very beginning," Dorothe said. "I mean, I never said anything bad to her. I never openly criticized her. But I did ask my questions although her attitude seemed to be that she did not want me to get involved with her work. That's the best way of putting it. She was handling it and I was just the mother. And there was no way I could add anything to this investigation."

One person I spoke to on condition of anonymity stated that Rubino did not come across as a force in the courtroom compared to the three slick lawyers for the defense, one of whom was the notorious Jack McMahon, Philadelphia's home-grown version of F. Lee Baily, who would scream and rant in the courtroom.

"First of all, Rubino was overweight whereas Jack McMahon was a force. It was 3 men against an overweight woman. When Rubino would walk up to the prosecutor's bench to the person giving testimony, she didn't have that sense of 'I'm in control.' Yet here was McMahon yelling and turning red in the face and shaking his fist."

While Dorothe believes that Rubino was a very good lawyer, she told me that she did not feel that she protected her daughter. "I didn't feel this, and that's what as a mother I wanted Judi to do, but obviously she was handling it and I asked questions that took up time but that's who I am, I ask questions, sometimes hard questions, but I'm not going to apologize.... I was a lady, I didn't swear, but I did not feel that she was a good match for the strong team on the defense."

On the other hand, Dorothe says she felt very comfortable with the detectives in whose company she says she "could say whatever I wanted to say." One of the things that the detectives told her was that McMahon had prostituted himself:

Yes, they used the word prostituted. I remember that because it shocked me, that McMahon had prostituted himself by contacting Richie Wise and Herbert Haak to represent them.... I guess you are not supposed to do that. McMahon at the time also wanted to run for DA. He kept the whole court waiting one day when we recessed for lunch and then came back and we had to wait until he finished his press conference. It was all publicity that he wanted for himself...

Dorothe said that McMahon had control of the court. And in a very strange confession, told me that Judge David N. Savitt had told her that he felt he had been too easy on the defense because he did not want the case to go into a mistrial. "I didn't want to put you through that," Dorothe says Savitt told her.

People, it seems, were always attempting to protect Dorothe—protect her from the horrors of the autopsy report, the stairwell, and from identifying her daughter's body in real time rather than on a computer screen. Now here was a judge telling her that he had gone too easy on the defense because he did not want to put her "through that," meaning the discombobulations of a mistrial. Nobody seemed to have a sense that Dorothe was a much stronger woman who only wanted the facts and the truth and that she could tolerate anything if it would bring justice for Kimberly. "A mother will do anything for her child."

In May 1997, *Philadelphia Magazine* published a long feature on Dorothe Ernest, titled "Mother of the Year." A significant part of the interview is devoted to Jack McMahon:

"I find it impossible to have one redeeming comment about Jack McMahon." This is Ernest's polite way of saying she hopes there is a special place in hell for Richie Wise's attorney, the current GOP candidate for district attorney. For her, the flamboyant lawyer represents everything that is wrong with the judicial system.

Mr. McMahon prostituted himself to get this case, claims Ernest. "He was talking about the case all over the press when Wise had another attorney. He poached big-time, got the case, and had a secret agenda in terms of his campaign."

For Ernest, who also expressed dismay at the defense's portrayal of the police and government as arch-villains, McMahon's greatest offense was his constant disrespect toward others in the courtroom. "He kept the court waiting while he held press conferences," claims Ernest. "Now, that is bad taste, lack of class and rude. How dare he hold up everybody. The jury might not have been sequestered as long if we hadn't always been waiting for Mr. McMahon. He shouted at the judge daily, shouted at witnesses. He'd turn his back when the judge was talking to him. He was just unbelievably rude."

Particularly galling was the treatment of her daughter's love life by McMahon. Prosecutor Judith Rubino called past lovers of Kimberly to the stand in order to suggest that semen found in her body, which did not match that of Haak or Wise, was the result of unprotected sex rather than of Kimberly being raped by her "real" attacker, as the defense claimed. At this juncture, McMahon claimed that the prosecution was dragging Kimberly's name through the mud in order to convict his client. Ernest was incensed.

"He had the audacity to accuse the prosecutor of not protecting Kim's name, and he was right up there drawing a vagina and an anus on the board and repeating his same sleazy questions over and over again," seethes Ernest. "He just talks out of both sides of his face."

In the *Philadelphia Magazine* interview, Ernest expresses frustration that lawyers are not held to the same standards of truthfulness that witnesses are. "I think lawyers shouldn't be allowed to lie to get their clients off. They should be sworn in just like witnesses. I mean, what is there role: to bring justice or just trick the jury?"

DAVID THE WEAK

"Judge Savitt's words did not sit very well for me!" Dorothe told me after revealing that the Judge went easy on the defense to protect her. Later, her detective friends would tell her that Savitt had the nickname, "David the Weak."

Dorothe would meet and talk with Judge Savitt sometime later when she returned to Philadelphia after attending her younger daughter's graduation from NYU.

She wrote the judge in advance and asked if she could make an appointment to see him, and that she would be happy to submit her questions in advance if that would help. "I really wanted to talk with him, so the meeting was set up. I thought, 'Oh he's going to be all formal and have his black robe on and sit behind his desk, and I'm going to sit in a little chair in front of his desk."

That is not what happened. Dorothe says that when the judge opened his door and welcomed her into his office, not only did he not have his black robe on, he had an Oxford button-down collar shirt on, open necked, "He was casual, and I started to go for the chair beside his desk and he said, 'No, no, no, let's sit over here on the couch.'"

To Dorothe, this meant that he was making it very clear that he was open and happy to answer any question she had. "He started the conversation when we sat down. He said: 'I just want to start off by saying, they are guilty, I know they're guilty.'" Dorothe says he told the judge, "That's not one of the questions I was going to ask you. My question was: Why did we lose this?"

"I just want to make it very clear that there was no doubt in my mind that they are guilty. I will be talking about this case for the rest of my career."

Dorothe challenged the judge. "I don't believe you when you say you'll be talking about this case for the rest of your career."

At that the judge stood up and walked to his desk, pulled open a file drawer, ruffled through a few letter files, and pulled out a stapled group of papers. "I'm going to be talking about this next month about how this was a very bad outcome."

Dorothe says that hearing the judge say this made her feel good. "I wanted someone to say that these guys are jerks," she said. The word jerks, of course, meant the two killers, Richie Wise and Herbert Haak. Dorothe's choice of the word to describe two ghastly killers was a vast underplay. "Jerk" was more *Willy Wonka and the Chocolate Factory* than a harsh condemnation, yet somehow it fits Dorothe's habit of always sounding like a lady.

She recounted how it was reported to her that the bailiff who escorted the jury to go into their meeting that first time heard one of the juror's say, "How long did it take the jury in the O.J. case? Let's see if we can beat it and come to a conclusion."

"This made me very sad," Dorothe said. But it was then that she understood these people were a sequestered jury. "They couldn't go home, they were in a hotel, they couldn't see their spouse, they couldn't see their children. They supposedly had a hard time making a decision as to what restaurant they were going to, so they often did carry out. Imagine not being able to decide which restaurant to go to—give me a break!"

The conversation returns to Kim's boss, Russ Cunningham. "He was overly kind to me," Dorothy recalled. "He was overly generous. I guess part of that was because he was a runner too. He talked to me and showed me where he wanted to put a sign on Kim's running route. You know, Kim was so funny. She was so proud when she could run up the steps like Rocky did at the Art Museum. She was proud that she could do this without stopping."

The police indicated to Dorothe that they suspected that a man in Kim's professional orbit was one of Kimberly's last lovers. It was a sticky situation. As Dorothe explained to me, "Because if the defense had learned that the prosecution had asked for DNA from somebody they thought was 'with' Kimberly, then they could always say, 'See, you are not certain that you got the right guys.' This still burns me," she says.

A night or two before Kimberly Ernest was murdered, Kim's friends told Dorothe that Kim was trying to contact them about a personal dating matter. "Kim was asking her friends, 'I really need to talk to you, I have a decision to make.' I think Kim was struggling whether she wanted to get involved with this man who had kids. They felt bad that they were not there for her. They were working. Anyway, that person she was deciding whether or not to date was coming over that night."

That night would have been November 1, 1995.

The conversation quickly turned to Kim's friends:

One of her friends was very close to Kim. She still contacts me although I don't contact her. I don't want her to feel obligated. Kim also loved to write letters. When you got a letter from Kim you could tell who it was from 30 feet away. She would decorate both sides of the envelope with magic markers, colors, designs and in the middle of all this would be the little clean white rectangle where she put the address. She also put things in the envelope that would sprinkle out when you opened the envelope. She had a joy for life. One could say that she took the road less traveled; she was her own unique person.

But, yes, when I think of that morning when she was jogging and met those two guys breaking into that car, I can easily see calling out and saying "Get away from that car. I'm going to call the cops."

THE LAST WEEKEND

"She was a wonderful older sister," Dorothe continued:

She took her 2 month old baby sister to Show and Tell in Kindergarten. I handed her this little tiny newborn baby—obviously I had to be right outside the door—but the two of them growing up were as tight and loving as two sisters could be. My friends would say, "How come your girls don't fight?" because their kids fought all the time.

The trick was there was a 5 ½ years difference between their ages, so there was no reason to fight, no rivalry. They were there for each other.

Dorothe tells me that Kim last saw her sister Sarah on Sunday night before Kim was killed on a Thursday, November 2:

Sarah was in New York City and took the train back and forth. Sarah visited Kim in Philadelphia that weekend. Kim was very concerned about Sarah being cold on the train on the way back to New York. Sarah recalls how concerned Kim was that she would be cold on the train. After Kim's death—and this is so sad—Sarah said to me, "How are we going to keep Kim warm now?"

When Sarah looked at me and said, "How are we going to keep Kim warm now," it grabbed my heart.

AFTERWORD

The AP reported that jurors needed less than a day to acquit Haak and Wise, with one juror admitting that the panel was convinced that police had lied and conspired to coerce the confessions. The trial was held not long after a Philadelphia Police Department two-year corruption scandal that led to the dismissal of more than 283 cases. One year before the trial, ten current and former police officers were charged with corruption, with six officers behind bars after pleading guilty to planting drugs on suspects and "shaking down drug dealers."

AP also reported that the city has paid more than $3.5 million in the past year to people who filed lawsuits, claiming they had been wrongly prosecuted and imprisoned as a result of corrupt officers

Jack McMahon, Philadelphia's thrift store version of F. Lee Bailey, was ecstatic. "As muck as Haak and Wise were on trial those police officers were also," he said. "This was a complete rejection of the government's case."

Other AP findings:

One juror said 11 members of the panel were ready to acquit within minutes of beginning deliberations Thursday. John Sutton, the lone holdout, said he relented, "even though I was letting down all the law-abiding citizens of Philadelphia."

Sutton says his fellow jurors were "convinced of police conspiracy, misconduct, lying perjury, forgery, everything else." Sutton himself was the subject of a jury note saying that there was "a problem with a juror who is threatening other jurors and also trying to provoke jurors."

Judge David Savitt dismissed the jurors curtly and without thanking them for their work during the month-long trial. Said McMahon, the defense attorney: "He clearly showed the jury he did not like the verdict."

In an article on police informants or "snitches," *The Philadelphia Inquirer* mentioned John Hall and his connection with the Kimberly Ernest case. "John Hall, seen under arrest in a 1994 file photograph, told authorities he obtained jailhouse confessions in numerous murder cases. He repeatedly received leniency for theft, drunken driving, and drug cases before his death in 2006."

Herbert Haak is currently a free man, and lives somewhere in the Fishtown section of Philadelphia.

Fred Ambrose's last two known addresses were in California and Florida.

Phyllis Hall is living in Philadelphia.

Thomas Joseph Augustine, former Philadelphia police officer and Homicide detective, passed away on Saturday, October 15, 2022. He was seventy-six years old.

A March 13, 1997 *New York Times* piece by Laura Mansnerus, "Doubts Haunt Philadelphia in Trial of 2 Men Charged in a Jogger's Murder," gets Kimberly Ernest's height wrong while alluding to the victim's active sex life and the high number of homicides in the city in 1995.

There were 432 homicides in Philadelphia in 1995, but just one that brought a teary tribute from the Mayor at the victim's memorial service.

That was the slaying of Kimberly Ernest, a 26-year-old paralegal who was attacked on her early morning jog through Center City in a crime that chilled that area's genteel row house blocks.

Throughout the city, talk of "the jogger murder" was instant, animated and practically ceaseless. Tensions eased only when, within a month of the crime, the police had confessions from two minor-league criminals who had apparently conducted a small crime wave in Center City around the time of the murder.

But however satisfying the confessions, they now turn out to be the only significant evidence against the men in their trial, which has gripped this city for the last few months.

The defendants contend that they were beaten and their statements fabricated by detectives, the elite in a department that since 1995 has seen more than 270 cases dismissed and six police officers imprisoned for extortion, planting evidence and lying in court. And as testimony concluded today, the city that demanded answers after the killing is caught between concerns that the guilty may go free and suspicions that the real killer is still out there.

"The lack of evidence is highly disturbing," said Stuart Seidman, a businessman, stating the common wisdom around Center City these days. "With all the corruption trials going on in the Philadelphia police, you'd think the cops wouldn't be dumb enough to blow this one. It's classic Philadelphia."

Ms. Ernest, a Chicago doctor's daughter, was killed about dawn on Nov. 2, 1995. She was found, in a bra, socks and running shoes, in a deep stairwell outside an office on Pine Street, near Rittenhouse Square.

An autopsy found that Ms. Ernest died of strangulation and blunt-force injuries to the head. There was evidence of rape: fresh vaginal tears, though no semen in the vagina, and traces of semen, though no sign of trauma, in the rectum.

In the next few weeks, the stairwell became a shrine, with flowers, candles and handwritten eulogies arrayed against the gate on the brick sidewalk. People gathered there to protest violence against women.

"This case is different," said Sgt. Paul Musi, who worked on the case. "For some reason, Philadelphia embraces this girl."

Fear and speculation dissipated with the arrests of Herbert Haak 3d, 25, a sometime computer repairman with a long list of burglary and theft convictions, and Richard Wise, an unemployed 19-year-old with a record of assaults. Mr. Haak lived with his fiancee in an apartment a few blocks from the crime scene, and Mr. Wise had been staying in an attached garage.

Mr. Haak called the police six days after the slaying. He was in jail in suburban Bucks County, where he had been detained after a court hearing on a burglary charge held within hours of Ms. Ernest's death. Mr. Haak told detectives that Mr. Wise was threatening to kill his fiancee; he also said Mr. Wise was involved in the Ernest killing.

The police picked up Mr. Wise for questioning, administering a polygraph test, which they said he failed. But having no other evidence, they released him.

A few weeks later, detectives heard from Mr. Haak's stepfather, John Hall, who implicated Mr. Haak along with Mr. Wise. Both men were arrested after giving confessions that told the following story:

Herbert Haak and Richard Wise, who had met as neighbors in Philadelphia's working-class Fishtown neighborhood, had a routine of breaking into cars and harassing people in the predawn hours around Center City. On Nov. 2, Mr. Haak was acting as lookout and Mr. Wise was approaching a parked car with a crowbar when Ms. Ernest, running down Pine Street, spotted him and threatened to call the police.

Mr. Wise hit her with the crowbar, but Ms. Ernest, 5 feet 10 inches tall and athletic, fought back. The men pushed her into their car, which was parked nearby, where Mr. Wise beat her into unconsciousness in the back seat and pulled off her pants while Mr. Haak drove, searching for a place to throw her out. They returned to Pine Street and dragged her into the stairwell. Mr. Wise tried to rape her but, he told the police, "I was just having a tough time trying to do it."

The wrenching story seemed to promise resolution. But investigators were soon brought up short. DNA from the semen in Ms. Ernest's body did not match either defendant. An examination of Mr. Haak's 1987 Bonneville yielded nothing, and while Mr. Haak's statement said they were driving a stolen car—Mr. Wise said they were in the Bonneville—the police could find no such car. There was no blood, no fingerprints, no crowbar, no witnesses. Ms. Ernest's pants were never found.

The trial, which began on Feb. 19 in Philadelphia Common Pleas Court, has produced a knot of ambiguous evidence. Mr. Haak's stepfather refused to testify, as did his mother, Phyllis, who had told police that Mr. Wise threatened to kill her if she revealed anything "about what we did to that girl."

It is not clear that Mr. Hall's testimony would have helped prosecutors; a habitual car thief, he is known as a jailhouse informer. The defense contends that to settle scores with his stepson he fed the police a story that detectives, under pressure to solve the case, used to fashion confessions.

At the trial, Mr. Wise never took the stand. Mr. Haak, however, testified to being beaten during his interrogation, and a prison social worker and a public defender said they saw red marks on his face and chest the next day. But three prison medical workers who saw him after the interrogation noted no signs of injury.

Mr. Haak also testified that detectives forced him to sign blank pages and that the confession must have been typed in later. But under cross-examination he was caught in many inconsistencies and acknowledged lying to a jury in a previous case. And in rebuttal testimony on Tuesday, a police documents expert displayed for jurors a magnified photo of a page of Mr. Haak's confession showing that a stroke of the defendant's signature had been placed on top of a typewritten line.

As to why he implicated Mr. Wise, Mr. Haak told the court that it was a ploy to get him out of his apartment and away from his fiancee.

Asked whether a false accusation of murder was not an overreaction, he replied: "I was trying to get police to go pick him up, so I was telling them anything I could think of."

One of Mr. Haak's fellow inmates testified that he had talked about "the wild man who lived in his garage" and who had "whacked" and raped the jogger; a former cellmate said Mr. Haak boasted that the car he and Mr. Wise had driven would never be found "because it was under water." But the jury also heard from inmates who questioned the cellmate's credibility.

Most confounding is the mystery sperm. The assistant medical examiner said it could have been a day or two old and the result of consensual sex. But he also said it could have been left by the killer, which would exclude both defendants.

Today, another prosecution expert said he believed that the sperm had resulted from vaginal intercourse more than a day before the assault.

Several of Ms. Ernest's friends and former lovers testified to her active sex life, but no one has acknowledged having sex with her in the days just before her death.

"They shouldn't be convicted on the evidence the police have," said Frank Bender, a sculptor who lives near Pine Street.

Still, Mr. Bender added, "I thought from the beginning they had the right guys."

A WEEK WITH HOMICIDE DETECTIVE TOM AUGUSTINE

On a weekday night around 10 p.m., the passenger drop-off area at Fort Lauderdale-Hollywood International Airport is pure bedlam. The parade of stop-and-go vehicles at Philadelphia International seems mild and controlled by comparison. Drivers honk relentlessly, even at slow grandparents picking up children and grandchildren.

Being Florida, it is a hot and steamy scene. The fast-forward movements in this pickup zone belie all stereotypes about the South being "slow." I feel like I have arrived in some South American country. Most people are not Caucasian like in Portland, Maine, or the Berkshires. I am reminded of the famous Seymour Krim book title from 1970: *Shake It for the World, Smartass.*

I am glad when my ride arrives.

Former Philadelphia Homicide Detective Tom Augustine, who interrogated Herbert Haak, arrested along with Richard Wise for the murder of Kimberly Ernest in November 1995, is now retired and lives in a lovely condo six floors up on a nice stretch of beach in Lauderdale-by-the-Sea. Tom, who experienced the worst of times when he worked in Philly, can handle pretty much anything except traffic.

"I hate to drive now," he tells me, after I put my suitcase on the back seat of his car. Of course, it is not the act of driving he hates (that being the sensation of fingers on a steering wheel) but the menace of other drivers—the rudeness, the ignorance, and the barbarity of what is happening on the road.

We are driving less than ten minutes when someone dashes in front of Tom and swerves to the left of the road and back again before engaging in a suicidal zigzag. All this happens on a road leading to a drawbridge over a canal that rises whenever a yacht needs to pass. Sometimes, depending on the time of day, there are more yachts and big boats than cars, so there is a lot of stalled traffic at the drawbridge. Tom tells me that years ago, before the city installed flashing lights to signal when the bridge was about to rise, a woman walker thought she could beat the drawbridge but miscalculated. "It's because of her death that we have the flashing lights," Tom said.

I think of her as we cross the bridge, wondering why she was in such a hurry.

It is 11:20 p.m. and most restaurants in Lauderdale-by-the-Sea are closed, so we opt for takeout from McDonald's to bring to Tom's condo. We sit in the kitchen. The sliding glass door that opens to his balcony is open, letting in a cool ocean breeze. Outside are palm trees, a world of difference from the honky-tonk and often trashy sounds of Aramingo Avenue in my Philadelphia neighborhood.

Who would not enjoy coffee and grapefruit juice on a balcony facing a beachfront—off season, no less—where one can spot—through Tom's binoculars—early morning swimmers and ships at sea? On a patio table, Tom has a baby rubber alligator that scares the pigeons that try to build nests on the condo balconies. In the balcony above his, deserted temporarily for the summer, a nest is already in progress. Management will not clean up a pigeon infestation if they see the beginnings of a nest, especially a nest with eggs. "It's got eggs," the security guy tells Tom when he calls to report virulent pigeon activity.

Staying out of the sun in an air-conditioned space is the goal of every southern Floridian. Tom's condo has a fairly large community pool with a deep end of 10 feet, a delight to swim in judging from the number of residents who hang out there for hours with their water noodles. By and large, the people who bask in the pool every day have skin types that allow them to do this. I do not, being a sunblock aficionado since the '70s.

Not far from Tom's condo is another condo high-rise where American flags are rarely flown. Is this because more Democrats live there?

The pool is a sort of community hub where information about residents is shared. Three days into my stay, I notice a recurring theme in Tom's stories about his neighbors. That theme is cancer. Everybody seems to have some form of cancer: cancer of the lung, brain, tongue, kidney, or cervix. Some have had chemo while others, freshly diagnosed, prepare for treatment as they take their daily swim. The high cancer rate seems to affect all ages, not just the ultra-retiree who may need a walker to get to the pool. Cancer is everywhere like the blue sky above the ocean.

It occurred to me that the high cancer rate in southern Florida may be more than coincidence, so I did a Google check and was hit by a landslide of headlines. Florida, I found, has the sixth-highest number of hazardous waste sites, known as Superfund sites, in the country. In 2016, the state was slated as having the second-largest number of new cancer cases in the country. *Science Daily* reported a relation between cancer and the Superfund sites. Florida also has the nation's third-highest cervical cancer rate, and cervical cancer mortality rate, in the country. There are also so-called "cancer hot spots" in Florida associated with hazardous waste sites. Brain cancer has been traced to radioactive water in the swamplands, and certain zip codes throughout the state have been pronounced "cancer clusters."

Since 2014, cancer has been the second leading cause of death in Florida after heart disease. What does this mean to the people in Tom's pool? Not much, I suppose, since, in their opinion, life is fragile and temporary (and you have to spend your time doing something). The people in Tom's condo, either cancer-diagnosed or cancer-free, live life to the fullest. Consider the retired Chicago stockbroker, a zillionaire, who goes to dialysis three times a week but who has a marvelous time when he takes a dip in the pool or the ocean. This makes me ponder: diagnosed with a fatal illness, would it be harder to "leave" life if you lived in what many consider to be paradise, as opposed to a ramshackle rowhouse in Port Richmond?

When it comes to love and romance, Fort Lauderdale has that in spades.

Quite a number of older men in Tom's complex are divorced but have younger second wives, many of them from Columbia. I cannot count how many times I heard the phrase, "He's an old guy, but you should see his young wife from Columbia!" It got me wondering whether there is a special Columbia-connected import/export dating business in Lauderdale. Even some women I was introduced to have first or second husbands from Columbia.

There are staunch liberals and conservatives in Tom's condo complex. Tom is conservative and flies his big American flag off his balcony whenever he can, but this practice has subjected him to criticism posing as "safety concerns." "Aren't you afraid that huge flag you fly will fall and hit somebody on the ground?" he was asked some months ago. The person asking this was a liberal Democrat, a woke retiree from Brooklyn. Not far from Tom's condo is the condo high-rise where American flags are rarely flown. I dubbed the condo "Charlie Crist's woke beehive" when Tom told me stories about some of the (unruly) occupants there.

Generally, the people in Tom's condo have learned to avoid politics as pastime conversation, but liberals being liberals, they sometimes cannot keep their mouths shut and will say things in the pool while fiddling with their noodles.

Tom's nearest neighbors are observant Orthodox Jews who often appear on their balcony in skull caps and prayer shawls. "Wonderful people," Tom told me. He says the same thing about his best friends, Carrie and Bill, a Russian Orthodox couple who live on the twelfth floor who invited us to a dinner party four days into my stay. Like serious Russian Orthodox believers, Carrie and Bill have a striking icon collection. They also make it a point to say grace before meals, something that has long gone out of fashion in society. As an Orthodox Christian, I asked what they thought of the Catholic Church of the Assumption, just across the street from their condo. I was told that the Mass there is somewhat "Protestant," especially when the Eucharistic ministers go pew to pew to distribute Holy Communion.

"Some people are so lazy they can't even walk up to the front of the church to take Communion," someone said. Of course, not all Catholic parishes are like this. Laziness ails Catholics and Orthodox, Protestants and Jews. Perhaps the parishioners' behavior can be traced to a nearby "cancer cluster."

Most days, I spent my time avoiding the midday sun and reading Jean-Luc Barre's *Beggars for Heaven*, the story of Jacques and Raissa Maritain. I would often walk the beach and take a dip into the ocean after 5 p.m. There was also a road trip with Carrie and Bill to Key Largo where we lunched in a thatched hut on the ocean's edge. Then there was church on Sunday—a small Orthodox congregation named Saint Nicholas.

In the evenings, I watched Sandra Bullock movies and a seven-part Andy Warhol documentary.

On my last day, Tom drove me to the airport at 5 a.m. where I boarded Flight 1004 for Philadelphia. I had a window seat and sat beside a professional surfer who had spent the last three months in El Salvador. His skin was brown as a berry, and he was so jetlagged he slept for the duration of the trip.

ABOUT THE AUTHOR

THOM NICKELS is a Philadelphia-based journalist/columnist and the 2005 recipient of the AIA Lewis Mumford Award for Architectural Journalism. He writes for *City Journal, New York, Frontpage Magazine, Broad and Liberty*, and the *Philadelphia Irish Edition*. He is the author of fifteen books, including *Philadelphia Architecture, Two Novellas: Walking Water & After All This* (the Lambda Literary Award finalist), *Out in History, Literary Philadelphia, Philadelphia Mansions*, and *From Mother Divine to the Corner Swami: Religious Cults in Philadelphia*. Nickels is the co-author of the play *Rendezvous in Bangkok: Who Killed Thomas Merton*, which had its premiere in 2022.